SITTO'S KITCHEN

A Treasury of Syrian Family Recipes
Taught from Mother to Daughter
for Over 100 Years

A Compilation of Sitto's Kitchen I and II in Full Color

Janice Jweid Reed

Acknowledgements

Photography by John Talley

Illustrations by Steven Galekovic

Edited by Herbert Schwarz

www.sittoskitchen.com

ISBN: 978-0-578-68935-7

This book is printed on acid-free paper.

Printed in the United States of America

Sitto Naima

I dedicate this cookbook to my grandmother, Sitto Naima, with belated thanks for all of her wonderful cooking and nurturing kindness throughout my childhood and young adulthood. She instilled in me my love of family, delicious Syrian foods and meaningful traditions. I think of her every time I pull out one of her recipes and I know she's there with me, in spirit, as I work the dough.

FOREWORD

This cookbook really began as a little spiral notebook, written with 26-year-old hands. At the time, I didn't realize I would want to make a book out of these recipes from my grandmother. I only wanted to learn how to make some of these wonderful Syrian foods. In those years, I saw cooking as a way to stay close to my grandparents' traditions. The culture and cuisine that I had so enjoyed while growing up were too precious to lose.

I hope that as you read bits and pieces of what I can remember, you'll get a glimpse of where my grandparents came from and the traditions our family brought with them from Aleppo, Syria, onto the shores of Ellis Island in 1912. This heritage has been lovingly carried into the 21st century by all of us who came after them, in our heads and in our hearts. This book is for all of them, but especially for my grandmother, Naima.

In 2000, I created an informal family cookbook for the children. Our family had grown more than I could have imagined so long ago and that cookbook was more important than ever in preserving the link of my grandparents' heritage for my children and their children.

In the next few years, as I spoke to young cooks, especially those of Arab ethnicity, I learned that many had not been fortunate enough to cook with their mothers or grandmothers. They reminded me of my own youthful inexperience and it prodded me to begin to create what you will now see. I hope those young beginners taste a little bit of "home" when they make these meals. I also hope that anyone new to Middle Eastern foods will be tempted to try these treasured dishes.

As I reflect back, I now realize that this collection of recipes has morphed from that little spiral notebook into a computer disk in the time it took for me to become a grandmother myself!

Author's Note, December 2016

A few years after publication of this cookbook, as I write this, my grandmother's beloved city of Aleppo is in ruins. After five years of war, millions are dead, injured or fleeing. And a once great city is unrecognizable.

I can't imagine leaving your home with only what you can carry, not knowing where you'll go, who will take you in, or if you will ever return. Are centuries of culture and family traditions soon to be lost? Will a once great culinary light in the Middle East shine no more?

I hope and pray the resiliency of the Syrian people will enable a return to their homeland and restore its greatness once more.

Author's Note, February 2020

This edited edition is a compilation of my first cookbook, Sitto's Kitchen and my second cookbook, Sitto's Kitchen II, the full color version with additional recipes. I hope that new readers and cooks will enjoy this as much as our fans have expressed so far. Follow me on Facebook and Pinterest for timely comment about these recipes along with input from our much-appreciated following!

TABLE OF CONTENTS

INTRODUCTION

My great grandmother and grandfather Kayal were shopkeepers in Aleppo, Syria. When great grandfather Nicholas died, great grandmother Amelia sent her two eldest sons, Naim and George, to America in hopes of easing their life. She later sent her eldest daughter, my grandmother Naima, accompanied by our friends, to join her brothers. Great grandmother promised she would soon follow with her remaining two daughters and two sons.

My grandmother Naima, whom I only called *Sitto*, meaning grandmother in Arabic, sometimes spoke of her trip across the ocean in August of 1912. She was just 14 years old, feeling alone and anxious about her journey and new life. She shuddered as she remembered that month aboard ship and being in the "belly of the ship." She remembered how sick the ocean had made them and believed they would perish as the ship tossed them about during a bad storm. She'd been on that ship with people speaking many languages, away from her family and the country she knew, wondering what lay ahead as they docked at Ellis Island, New York.

I learned my grandmother's history in bits and pieces during our life together. She had married as a young girl of 15 to my grandfather, Bashir. Her two brothers, Naim and George, soon married after arriving in America as well. Great grandmother, Amelia, "Mellau," arrived a few years later with her daughters Zekeya and Jamila. The two remaining sons, Aboud and Antoun remained in Syria at this time. The family was all settled in Paterson, New Jersey, by 1918. Within the next several years my grandparents produced four sons and a daughter, my mother, Mary.

Many other Syrian and Lebanese immigrants began arriving in Paterson, New Jersey, in the early 20th century. The textile industry was burgeoning in this growing city. Ready work was available for them upon their arrival. My own family worked in those mills.

These Syrian immigrants did not have their Eastern Melkite Church or its priests when they first arrived. It wasn't until 1920 that the Melkite community began meeting for worship in the basement of nearby St. Michael's Italian Church. It had to have been a unique melding of these two Mediterranean cultures.

In June 1922, the Aleppo parishioners began working towards a plan to build their own church in the Syrian colony they were forming. This proposed new church began as a temporary hall in the hopes that they could finish the building once the parishioners had saved enough money. The hall was built and dedicated by December 8th. However, as the years passed, the Great Depression had hit the community. With many of the men out of work, an incredible undertaking began. These unemployed, impoverished immigrants would complete their own church. So, beginning in 1930, the amateur construction crew, led by their parish priest, Father Anid, acting as general contractor, began building the shell of the new church, employing these parishioners on a rotating basis. His plan would help employ the community's families while building for their future church. The new walls were actually built around the walls of this temporary hall they had used for worship during this time. As the new walls were completed, the old building's walls were torn down. To save the labor and cost of hauling the demolished temporary structure away, the men buried it beneath the floor of the new building. The parishioners erected the massive and beautifully designed dome by 1932. St. Ann's Melkite Catholic Church became an impressive landmark in Paterson and was dedicated in 1932, ten years after the dedication of the temporary hall that was my grandparents' first place of worship here in America.

The community continued to grow and even managed to thrive between the period of the Great Depression and World War II. Paterson was filled with many Syrian and Lebanese families, shops and markets and, just as it was in Syria, the homes and businesses were all centered around their church. This community continues to this day and I reflect, with pride, that my grandparents were among the earliest parishioners of this great church. Although the magnificent old church tragically burned down in 1972, the newly built church now located in Woodland Park, New Jersey, is still the anchor for this vibrant Syrian-American colony.

At the time, St. Ann's Church was fast becoming the hub of the Syrian and Lebanese community. Its parishioners celebrated their religious holidays, summer festivals or *Mahrajans* and winter galas or *Haflas*, all welcoming their growing and recently arrived families. Later, as I grew up in that community, with our relatives and friends all nearby, I too was immersed in our culture and had a great sense of belonging.

My grandmother, Sitto Naima, was always there for us as my sister and I would come home from school to these ethnic foods, breads and the sweets she made. It was in these adolescent and teen years that I gained my moral compass, my love of tradition, and my admiration for the incredible Syrian cooking all around me through the example of my grandmother.

In later years, as a young married woman, I found myself moving to the Midwest. I was just twenty-six years old and, for the first time, off to a new place with my husband and our three very young children. Family, friends and the Syrian community I grew up with were all left far behind. Like a college student away from home, I suddenly became aware of all the ethnic cooking I couldn't produce and had only watched my grandmother make. I knew, all too well, if I wanted to give my children any kind of a heritage, I had better start preparing these dishes.

I began to telephone my grandmother and ask for advice on how to make this or that. This prompted me to start a journal in which I painstakingly transformed her "handful of this" to a half-cup of that. In time, my simple spiral notebook caught the fruits of my own labors. Her recipes, scratched out here and there with revisions or corrections and little slips of paper that were Sitto's instructions, were the real start of this cookbook. During those years, she and my mother would send packets of spices that were unavailable to me in the Midwest. These "care packages" would always be accompanied by a note, written by my mother, with my grandmother's advice on how much spice to use in a dish. Those precious notes were a piece of "home," encouraging me to emulate those dishes I missed so much.

My husband's grandparents, who also emigrated from Syria, provided some wonderful recipes as well. I began to work side-by-side with my mother-in-law, Mary, on her visits to the Midwest and some of her recipes are included in my journal. She was a superb cook, very different from my grandmother, who was more frugal with meat and butter portions. I now see that my grandmother's generation was right and that many of the dishes containing a few ounces of meat were far more healthful than any of us realized at the time. Sitto always planned her meals with vegetables first, always buying what was in season.

So, over a period of years, I wrote down these recipes in my little spiral notebook. These wonderful dishes had been passed on from great grandmothers and mothers-in-law to family cooks as part of their daily lives. Thankfully, I was able to perfect these recipes while still able to ask these talented cooks for advice.

Many of the recipes I've collected and remembered are centered around a holiday or religious feast day. All of these foods have a tradition that was the backbone of the menu. Seasons, events and local customs all dictated what was served to the family, like a wonderful yogurt salad served at Easter to signal spring. As a youngster, I loved a wheat confection called Sleetah, which was served to honor St. Barbara's feast day in December, complete with the song we all sung about her martyrdom. Wonderful appetizers or *Mezze*, which would be served for guests, were healthful, colorful and nutritious.

Every time I open a jar of dried mint flakes, another memory of my grandmother comes to mind. Her use of mint, to make her basic spice paste for stuffed grape leaves or squash, would have her reaching for her heavy, well-worn

My Notebook

brass mortar and pestle. She'd pound the coarse salt and garlic until pureed and then add the dried mint flakes to make a paste of these basic ingredients. In fact, all of her ground spices were to be pounded at one time or another in the old brass mortar and pestle, her *Hehwan*, brought from Syria. I remember how she relied upon it as I use it in my kitchen today. I sometimes use my garlic press or blender when rushed but, I must say, the mortar and pestle is by far a more authentic blending of the spices and garlic, infusing all these dishes with a deeper, richer flavor.

Recipes that are not in this book also prompted me to think about saving these 100-year-old family recipes, like my husband's grandmother Jaleela's elusive sponge cake. My husband had such wonderful memories of that simple homey cake and wished for it many times. None of us could ever recapture it. But then again, Jaleela was so much her own person; her cooking had to be as unique. Colorful and endearing Sitto Jaleela kept her artificial Christmas tree, fully decorated, in her hall closet and whipped it out every Christmas, as proud as could be that she was all ready for the holidays!

I remember my Sitto Naima's candied orange, grapefruit and eggplant…the baby eggplant was hollowed out, sugared and crunchy with a wonderful walnut filling. She made these delicacies when I was very young. When I asked her about it years later, she claimed it was too much work in the earlier years and then later said she had forgotten how to make it.

Other forgotten wonders of the kitchen, prepared by Sitto Naima, were the wonderful dried meats called *Ehdeed*. I never got the recipe, but I remember her preparing the meat with a spice rub, wrapping it in cheesecloth, and then putting it on the clothesline until the cured meat was ready to be sliced and eaten. My mother-in-law Mary's "Damson plum preserves" are another delectable memory. As much as I followed her around writing down recipes, this one I never got. There are other terrific examples of ethnic cooking that I sampled at relatives' homes in Paterson and Brooklyn, New York, that I never wrote down and could never duplicate.

Young cooks, please take note. No matter how carefully someone in your family may try to impart what they know about a dish, some of it will be lost. Over the years, I've found that the nuances of cooking are very much owed to the particular cook. That's why the act of being side-by-side with your mom, aunt or grandmother is so very special. That handful of herbs, the feel of the dough, the particular look of the dish as it simmers or thickens, can only be learned through experience. How better to experience it than with the one who nourishes you with their lovingly made dishes?

And the stories! Each dish reminds the cook of his or her own childhood, of aromas and tastes that are long gone, memories faded but not forgotten. These traditions are the best ingredient you can put into your cooking. It is for this reason that I recorded and practiced and hopefully passed on to my children and their children. It is, in part, a genealogy that traces our ethnic roots, our religious beliefs and traditions, even our family's idiosyncrasies. The very ingredients show us the influences of the society and times in which we lived.

Oh how I miss that little kitchen which had its roots generations ago, in Aleppo, Syria. I picture my Sitto, always in her magical kitchen, preparing one thing or another, stirring a fragrant dish or baking bread. As I came in from school, I remember the wonderful aromas of the day, garlicky or sweet smelling, redolent with spices in the air. To me, it meant love for her family and our heritage.

Now that I'm far away in California, I have a deep sense of loss for my community and the Arabic language that slipped so easily off my tongue in those days. I reflect on the niceties of greeting our Syrian guests with blessings of hospitality. We were always taught to say "*Salame*," "welcome to our home," to each of our visitors. "*Allah Salmak*," "God bless you," would be the reply. Syrian households catered to their guests and as a youngster I'd be asked to say "*Fudalu*" as I offered a homemade treat. Today I am still so conscious of my guests' comfort at our gatherings and realize those early lessons from my grandmother influenced me later in life. As I write this, it's clearer that she is still with me as I carry that gentility in my heart. The memory is fading, but never my love for my Sitto, who showed me the way. I hope, in some small way, that I can leave that behind for my grandchildren and their children. They should know where they came from and the loving cooks who came before them.

The recipes remain as a reminder of our Syrian family's heritage and the devoted cooks who preceded us. It is through the cooking that my grandmother and the others live. Each time I prepare a dish, I remember my first try at it, my grandmother's words of advice or reproval and her spirit is with me as I work the dough for yet another generation. That is my grandmother's legacy.

Syrian Cultural Heritage

STOCKING THE SYRIAN COOK'S KITCHEN

The recipes in this book are compiled from more than one hundred years of traditional Arab cooking. They have been translated from mother to daughter, mostly from memory and carried through tradition because the Syrian cook has always had great pride in her kitchen abilities. Each mother imparts that pride as they show their daughters, by example, how to prepare the meals their own mothers taught them. Today, the cuisine of Aleppo, Syria, is considered one of the best of the Middle East.

Those of us in more modern times have been sometimes frustrated because there are no cookbooks telling us how much of this or that is in a family recipe. In trying to emulate my grandmother's recipes, especially at the long distance I was at the time I compiled the beginnings of this book, I would often have to repeatedly ask her for more detail. Her generation was very fond of giving ratios. A pound of this would mean two pounds of that. And the spices and herbs would be a pinch of this, a handful of that. As I compiled these recipes, I refined, called my grandmother with more questions, and refined again. There were comical errors in my younger days and now I see, as a grandmother myself, that many years of cooking only helps you to forget how literal you should be in your instructions. So, even today, as I prepared this cookbook, I became more and more literal, as I thought of the younger cook, wishing to emulate the old-timer's recipes with modern conveniences.

Much can be lost through those years of traditional cooking. And conversely, much can be gleaned and then simplified. Many of the recipes can now be shortened because of kitchen conveniences such as electric mixers, blenders, food processors, sausage attachments, juicers, spice grinders and such. The availability of produce year round, meats from the U.S., New Zealand, and abroad allow today's cook more versatility. While the pluses outweigh the minuses, there is something to be said for the traditional ways of preparing these century-old recipes. I will attempt to note these recipes with tips where necessary. For now, the basics of the Syrian cook's kitchen are as follows:

Meats: Lamb was used exclusively, mostly from the lean leg meat, and ground twice for *Kibbe* or ground once, with some fat, for other dishes. Middle Eastern markets and some supermarkets provide lamb. If the supermarket is your only option, look for ground lamb and grind it again at home in a food processor or mixer with a grinder attachment. I have used beef as a substitute and it can sometimes be accomplished with similar results. I have noted where these substitutions will work in each recipe.

Kitchenware: The Syrian cook traditionally used a heavy brass mortar and pestle to puree garlic, salt, mint and/or spices into a paste or powder. I have found these in Middle Eastern stores. In modernizing my grandmother's recipes, I have suggested a blender or spice grinder, food processor and garlic press where possible. I can attest, however, that the pureed spice paste from a mortar and pestle is immeasurably better in infusing and enhancing a dish like the original.

Pots and pans are typical of any well-stocked kitchen. Baking pans should be of heavy-duty, good quality, with a lip all around. Generous 7 to 10 quart-pots and assorted pans can all be found in any good kitchen store. A small and large skillet, saucepans, flat metal skewers, and standard wooden and metal kitchen cooking utensils will work well. Large round and rectangular baking pans, even a pizza stone for baking bread, will all be helpful in preparing these

Mortar & Pestle, Mahshi and Sausage Tools

foods. Most recipes will state any special handling or equipment needed.

Some specialty implements will be found in Middle Eastern stores in your town or on-line. For coring squash, the traditional two-sided, long-handled, slimmer u-shaped corer called a *Ma'Wara* is readily available in Middle Eastern stores. For pastries, the specialized *Mahmoul* mold, resembling a deeper butter mold is ideal. For *Aros*, a pastry wheel and imprinted blocks are available at Middle Eastern stores or alternatives can be used. Suggestions would be the pasta or ravioli wheel to seal the turnovers. A new printing block would work well for the imprinting of the tops of the *Aros* turnovers. For the traditional *Ejjeh* omelets, I have found that the Danish Ebelskiver pans available at quality kitchen stores are a close second. They have round indentations for filled puffy pancakes and make a good alternative for the mini *Ejjeh* omelets. Each recipe will suggest modern alternatives that can be purchased on-line or in some local areas.

Many of the dry ingredients are available on-line in Middle Eastern markets. If you are lucky enough to live in an urban area with ethnic neighborhoods, shopping for grains should be easy to accomplish at these or at health food stores in your area.

Aleppo's trade route had a profound effect on its cooking traditions and exotic spices, seeds and herbs became an integral part of its cuisine. The Glossary will be helpful in stocking the pantry with the appropriate spices, grains, legumes, nuts and flavorings.

The overall Middle Eastern diet is a healthy one, rich in vegetables and grains, colorful and honestly easy to make with today's modern appliances. I can't help but think that my ancestors would be amazed with the ease of preparation in which their dishes can now be made. I hope you enjoy emulating these wonderful old recipes with the same love that the Syrian cook has always had for her family. Hearty appetite! *Bil Hana!*

Spoons

THE BASICS

There are several recipes that are basic and typical of the Syrian cook's staples. For this reason, I have put these recipes in one section, as a referral. Bread dough, clarified butter, yogurt, sugar syrup and tamarind syrup will be the most used and most important ingredient in many of these recipes. You'll find that they will also become a staple your family enjoys.

My grandmother, Sitto Naima, like all those Syrian cooks before her, didn't have a written recipe for anything…just those memories from cooking alongside her mother or grandmother, and later, her mother-in-law. What was remarkable about my grandmother was her organization, her years of skilled timing, her multi-tasking (even before it had a name) and the precision with which she prepared a dish. These were learned through experience and having watched her own parents and grandparents as they worked with her. And so, I thought I'd try to remember tips, both verbal and subliminal, given to me by my Sitto:

Sitto always weighed her ingredients and her kitchen scale was nearby and used often. Her instructions to me were always in ratios; for instance, "5 pounds of flour to a pound of semolina and a pound of clarified butter." I thought it "old-fashioned" but when I was putting my notebook together, I would write exactly as she said. As I later wrote the recipes for the cookbook, I laboriously translated it to cups or ounces, thinking it the easier method for today's reader. Much later, I read tips from several chefs who advised that weighing rather than measuring by volume improves the finished product. It made sense as I realized that semolina grains surely are different in volume than flour. And then I knew that Sitto was right all along!

I remember a time, as Sitto was making Syrian String cheese, she prepared her brine of salt and water, never measuring, just using her experience to know the ratio. She would take an egg from the carton, still in its shell, gently placing it into the water. I watched in wonder as she told me that if it floated to the surface, to the size of a quarter, the salt-to-water ratio was good!

Watching Sitto prepare her dough for bread or any pastry, she'd pull out her baking sheets. No, they were not cookie sheets. They were old, worn, freshly laundered bed sheets! She would place them on the kitchen table. When the dough had been kneaded and ready to "rest and rise," she'd place those dough mounds on the sheets and then cover them with more sheets, preventing any drafts to ruin the yeast. The internal "heat" generated would allow the dough to rise beautifully. Today, I do the same. And, it's kind to the environment, no foils, wax papers, parchment papers are necessary!

In Sitto's kitchen, there was not a glass jar that ever went to waste. She would scrub them clean and "recycle" them for spices, her homemade syrups and jams, pickled turnips and cauliflower, anything she needed. And I agree. Today, I reuse all of these jars. Again, kind to the environment.

Back in the 50's, Sitto covered her leftovers with little plastic caps. It was the method of the day. She'd wash them and reuse them. Today, I noticed they are coming back!

Things I learned through the years, that I didn't know as a young cook, are of course, many. But one important discovery may be the only one you need to remember. Read any recipe before shopping for it and then again before actually preparing it. The reason is that often the ingredients list something like "sliced carrots." That would mean that the carrots should be peeled and sliced and ready. So, through the years, I realized that having those items prepared at the start of the recipe made quick work of the whole task. It made it much less of a challenge, allowed me to time things better and left me a lot less stressed. To this day, I place all of the ingredients before me to confirm that I actually have them or have the right amount.

Another tip is to place your prepared, measured or opened ingredients into separate small dishes or bowls. For instance, if you are asked to add eggs into a recipe, never open them directly into the dish you are making. As a young cook, I remember my surprise in cracking a few eggs into a batter, only to find that one of them was spoiled. Of course, the whole batter had to be tossed. So, those little prep dishes you see professional chefs have lined up before starting a dish are not just for convenience. They'll ensure that you have ample and fresh ingredients already sliced and diced. Since these recipes list the ingredients as they are used, even pulling out the measuring cups and spoons, pots or sauté pans, cutting board and knives help you follow the recipe in a quicker and more orderly fashion.

Another good reason for reading these recipes through is that I have found some recipes can be partially prepared a day ahead. In the case of working cooks, it's always helpful to be able to "prep" by preparing some of the recipe on a day when you have more time. Some recipes need a pre-chilling or marinating and can be thought out and prepared in advance.

Not one of these recipes is difficult, although some may be more challenging than others. I hope I have made the instructions clear. I first tried these recipes as a very young woman, with no prior cooking experience, and you will surely be able to as well. May these delicious foods be enjoyed by your family and welcome your guests for years to come. *Ahlan Wa' Sahlan!*

Sitto's Pots, Pans, Mortar & Pestle

It was typical of our community that we always helped our family and friends who wanted to immigrate to America, often, just one or two at a time. When I was in my late teens, my grandmother wanted to help the Fattal family by giving young George, newly arrived from Aleppo, a "home-away-from-home." George lived with her for a few years, until his parents and other siblings could join him. When the family did arrive, they opened a little bakery in the heart of South Paterson. Today, many years later, their business is an institution in that Middle Eastern neighborhood. The store is always crowded with customers from the neighborhood, as well as those who travel from their suburban homes to pick up their delectable Syrian bread, pastries, meats and staples for the Arab table. When I go into the store, I always have to smile as I think back to those early days when this young immigrant family got their start in their new country, and what part my Sitto Naima played in it.

SYRIAN BREAD
KHUBIZ SHAMI

1	PACKAGE DRY YEAST
1/2	TEASPOON SUGAR
2	CUPS WARM WATER (DIVIDED USE)
4	CUPS ALL PURPOSE FLOUR
1	TABLESPOON SALT
3	TABLESPOONS OIL (DIVIDED USE)
	ADDITIONAL FLOUR, AS NEEDED

Syrian Bread

Dissolve the yeast and sugar in a cup of the warm water. Blend and set aside for 5 minutes until bubbly. Add 2 Tablespoons oil.

Pour the flour into a large 4 qt. bowl, add the salt and mix through. Leave a well in the center and then add the yeast mixture into the flour and mix. Gradually continue with the water while beginning to knead. You may not need all of the water. Add flour to your hands, if needed. You may need to add an additional cup of flour if it is still sticky. On a floured board, knead for about 10 minutes, or until dough appears to be smooth and elastic.

Coat the bowl with the remaining oil, turning the dough over to coat the top with the oil to keep it from drying out. Cover the dough with plastic wrap and leave in a warm, draft-free place to rise, about 1 1/2 hours, until doubled in bulk. I use my cold oven with the light turned on.

When the dough has doubled, punch it down and knead for a few minutes. Then pinch off equal-sized balls, 3" in diameter. Place them on a floured work surface such as clean, thin cotton sheets, parchment or waxed paper. Flatten the balls with your fingers or a rolling pin all around and make them about 1/4" thick by about 6" to 7" in diameter, depending on how large you would like them. Cover the rounds with a cloth and let them rise again for about 45 minutes.

While they rise, place a seasoned pizza stone on the lowest rack to heat and preheat the oven to 500 degrees.

If a pizza stone is not available, use any heavy duty baking sheet, and preheat the sheet for just a few minutes before putting the bread rounds on it.

Place the dough rounds on the stone and bake for approximately 3 minutes. The timing depends on your oven. When baked, they will puff up and will be golden on top and lighter on the bottom.

Place them on a clean cloth and then cover the breads as they come out of the oven with another cloth. Do not stack them. The breads will be soft and two-layered inside, like a pita pocket. Place in plastic bags while still warm. Makes about 8 rounds.

Cook's Notes: Like my grandmother, have a bowl of water handy, and dip your fingers into it and splash the bread tops if they are browning too much. My grandmother would sometimes slip them under the broiler for a few seconds for color if, conversely, they aren't browning. Since ovens differ, this may vary.

In working with the dough rounds as they rise, I have used waxed or parchment paper taped down on my counter top and then lightly floured. However, my grandmother's way seems to be best. If you reserve thin, clean cotton sheets, which may have worn over time, and use these sheets only for baking, you'll have an easier time with the breads and the flouring. It seems modern kitchens can't improve on a good idea.

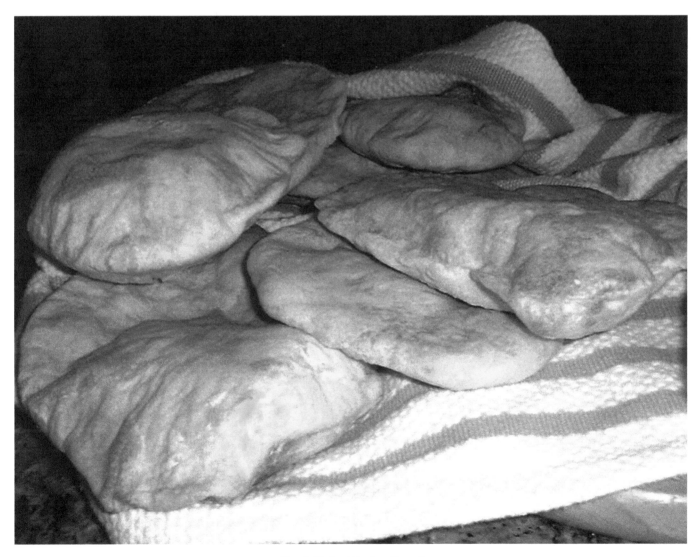

Fresh Baked Syrian Bread

This Simple Syrup is the basis for so many Syrian sweets. For this reason, it is considered basic. You'll find that having it in your refrigerator will allow a quick turn-around for so many of these sweets and beverages.

SUGAR SYRUP
SHIRREH

4	**CUPS SUGAR**
1 1/2	**CUPS WATER**
1/2	**LEMON OR A DASH OF LEMON SALT (SEE GLOSSARY)**
1	**TABLESPOON ORANGE BLOSSOM WATER (MAHZAHAD)**

Dissolve the sugar in the water and bring to a boil in a medium 2 qt. saucepan. Cover and lower the heat to a simmer for about 5 minutes. Uncover and squeeze the half lemon or lemon salt into the mixture and stir to prevent crystallization of the syrup. Simmer uncovered for an additional 10 minutes.

Test a drop of the mixture on a plate to cool. The mixture should be syrupy and slightly thickened. It will thicken more when it's cold. In the last few minutes before removing from the heat, add the Orange Blossom Water flavoring, stirring to blend the flavoring throughout and remove from the heat.

Pour into a glass container to cool. Makes 3 1/2 cups. Serve at room temperature or as each recipe stipulates.

The syrup will serve you well, covered and stored in the refrigerator for up to 2 months. It can be used in many traditional Syrian recipes. Having it on hand will help immeasurably in making these recipes much quicker.

Cook's Notes: The simmer time can vary depending on the thickness of the syrup desired. If the syrup is too thick, more water may be added.

Don't stir during the second simmer or as you pour into a container. The sides of the pan will be crystallized.

The amount of Orange Blossom Water will depend upon your taste and whether the brand is potent or not. Rose Water may be used as an alternative to the Orange Blossom Water.

Lemon salt, also known as citric acid, is available in Middle Eastern markets and on-line through spice merchants.

The basic recipe for clarified butter is used in many of our Syrian sweets. It is not to be confused with sweet butter as that won't work in many recipes. I know, because in my younger days, I tried it! Aside from its traditional use in many of the pastries, it will not burn in recipes calling for frying or sautéing. Clarified butter keeps for a long time, covered and refrigerated.

CLARIFIED BUTTER
ZIBDI M'DATAHA

2   **LBS. SALTED BUTTER**

Melt butter slowly in a medium 3 qt. saucepan, bringing to a simmer, without stirring, for about 30 minutes.

A foam residue will rise to the top. This is the salt and milk solids, which should be skimmed from the surface as it simmers.

Skim the butter without stirring or disturbing the amber-like liquid below it.

After all the foam has been skimmed, and the butter appears clear and without a skin-like sediment on top, remove from the heat and allow to cool.

When it cools to room temperature, pour into a glass measuring cup using only the amber clarified butter and leaving the bottom sediment undisturbed and to be discarded. This should yield about 2 1/2 to 3 cups of butter. The butter can be refrigerated for another time or after reaching room temperature, it can be used in any other recipe calling for clarified butter.

Cook's Notes: When a recipe specifies clarified butter, it will only produce the right result if it is used. When a recipe specifies sweet butter, it can be melted and used as the shortening, without the need to clarify it. If a recipe specifies butter, consider it salted.

More or less of the butter in this basic recipe may be used, depending on the particular recipes in this book. Since clarified butter will keep for several weeks in the refrigerator, well covered, this amount will serve you well for one or more recipes.

One of my earliest recollections of my grandmother are the wonderful bites of yogurt and homemade bread that she lovingly hand-fed me as a toddler. I always loved how creamy and tangy her homemade version tasted. Years later, I watched as she made the yogurt and let it sit on the stovetop, in what seemed like magic, to become one of our family's staples. And as a teen, I had to be reminded not to take the last bit of yogurt in the refrigerator so that she could use it as the starter for her new batch!

YOGURT
LABAN

1	QT. WHOLE MILK
4	TABLESPOONS PLAIN ORGANIC YOGURT (TO BE USED AS THE "STARTER")

Heat the milk in a 2 qt. saucepan, just to a boil. Then lower to a simmer for 2 to 3 minutes. Remove from the heat to cool.

While the milk cools, take the yogurt "starter" and mix it in a medium 2 qt. bowl until it is liquified. Set aside.

Remove any skin that has formed on the top of the hot milk and discard.

The traditional way to test the hot milk for readiness: If you could leave your finger in it to the count of ten, it was ready to add to the starter.

The modern method to test: Use an instant-read thermometer. When it reads 118 to 120 degrees, the milk is ready to mix into the starter.

Pour a few tablespoons of the milk, at a time, into the starter, beating vigorously to blend. Then add the rest of the milk, continuing to beat until well blended.

Cover the bowl with plastic wrap. Wrap with a towel and leave in a warm place for about 8 hours or longer. When the yogurt is solid, refrigerate.

Cook's Notes: For the starter, be sure to use yogurt with live cultures.

Once the milk begins to cool, watch it closely, as the temperature can go from too hot to too cool quickly.

My trick for developing the yogurt is to keep the wrapped bowl in my cold oven with the light on. It's the closest I can get to my grandmother's trick of keeping it on the pilot light of her stovetop. Yogurt is easy and much more healthful when homemade with no sugars, fruits or chemicals. It will have a thick, tart and distinctly rich taste!

TAMARIND SYRUP - A STAPLE OF ALEPPO'S COOKS

Tamarind Pods

As a young married woman, I made this syrup with my mother-in-law, Mary, and included it in my journal cookbook. Remembering back on that day so long ago, I had never even seen tamarind before. She called it Tamar Hindi, literally meaning Indian Date in Arabic, perhaps from the date-like appearance of the pods. It was strange looking, with curved, brown, bean-like pods hanging from the branches. The pod, about five inches long, contained a sticky reddish-brown edible pulp enclosed around several shiny brown-black seeds. It was the pulp, however, that we needed to start our syrup. After soaking this strange mass of pods, stems and fibrous husks overnight, we placed them into a colander within a large bowl. We then squeezed the pods and seeds allowing the juicy pulp to strain through the colander. Then we captured the remaining pulp and juice through a finer sieve. We followed the recipe below and proceeded to simmer the puree for several hours until the consistency of thick syrup.

Both my grandmother and mother-in-law referred to this syrup as Dibis Rumman, although technically, "Rumman" means pomegranate in Arabic. The reason for this is that some cooks used the pomegranate juice along with the tamarind for their syrup and I've included their versions. Many Arab cooks rely on the pomegranate syrup alone and I have found many regional recipes using just this syrup. Although I've tried these commercial jars, they are no substitute for the tangy, sweet/sour accent that tamarind gives these authentic Aleppo dishes.

I later discovered that tamarind is also used in many Indian, Hispanic and Asian foods. Aleppo, Syria is an old trade route and it's very possible that tamarind's origin in our dishes had an Indian influence. Tamarind's natural pectin is also used in many commercial jams and jellies and is the ingredient for a popular Middle Eastern drink.

Aside from the fresh pods, which are always found in Hispanic food stores, you can now purchase wet or slab tamarind, also known as block tamarind, at many Middle Eastern or Indian food stores. Concentrated tamarind paste is another option that is also available in jars, which shortcuts the pod or block methods of preparation.

For the purposes of showing the alternate methods of preparing this syrup, and to allow a reader to choose the most convenient, I have presented four other versions of the basic recipe. Thankfully, this may eliminate all of the steps my grandmother and even my mother-in-law took in their day. The original recipe is still there for those of us who are purists and want to keep the traditional recipe on the record. Whichever version you choose to make in order to have this basic condiment syrup in your pantry will definitely qualify you as an Aleppo cook!

MARY JWEID'S ORIGINAL TAMARIND SYRUP
DIBIS TAMAR HINDI MIN MARY JWEID

6	LBS. TAMARIND PODS (TAMAR HINDI)
1	32 OZ. BOTTLE LEMON JUICE CONCENTRATE OR JUICE OF 20 LEMONS
2	CUPS WATER
6	LBS. SUGAR
2	TABLESPOONS LEMON SALT (SEE GLOSSARY)
1	16 OZ. JAR CAROB JAM, OPTIONAL (SEE COOK'S NOTES)

Step 1: Place the tamarind pods into a large 4 qt. bowl and rinse a few times with cold water to remove any surface residue. Peel and rinse again. Cover the fruit with fresh, cold water and soak overnight.

Step 2: The next day, drain the water out. Place the softened tamarind into a colander and rinse out the bowl. Place the colander back into the bowl. Squeeze the pods, crushing them to release the sticky paste. Gradually pour the lemon juice and 2 cups of water over your fingers and through the seeds and fibers as you continue to squeeze in order to facilitate this process. Any remaining pulp will be eased through. Remove the colander and discard the stems, seeds and fibers.

Step 3: Place a fine strainer or sieve over another large bowl and press the pulp through the strainer, using a wooden spoon to facilitate it. Rinse the other large bowl and the sieve. Repeat this process through the sieve again. This may need a third run through the sieve or through cheesecloth, depending on any tiny particles that remain. When the pulp appears smooth, without dark specks of shell, continue to the next step.

Step 4: Pour the strained mixture into a large 6 qt. non-aluminum pot and bring to a boil. Then lower to a simmer. Stir occasionally, using a wooden or non-metal spoon, until it begins to reduce and thicken somewhat. Then add the sugar and the lemon salt and continue to simmer until it darkens further and is a syrup consistency, much like molasses. Taste for tartness and adjust if necessary during this simmer.

Check your progress by placing a tablespoon of the syrup on a plate, to let it cool. If it is the consistency of molasses, it is ready to remove from the heat. Average overall simmer: Approximately 3 to 4 hours.

Let the mixture cool and then pour into clean glass jars and store in a cool, dry place for up to 18 months. There is no need to refrigerate this syrup. This recipe makes about 4 to 5 cups.

Cook's Notes: My mother-in-law told me that she would sometimes add a jar of carob molasses along with the sugar. At the time we made this recipe, we did not add it because we couldn't get it locally. Her syrup was wonderful and I would suggest trying it either way.

The only thing to watch for is that the syrup tends to billow up when stirred towards the end of the simmer. Stir occasionally and with caution and keep the heat low to avoid a spillover. I recommend a stovetop diffuser for such a long simmer. This prevents scorching of the pan and the heat will be diffused and more consistent.

My mother had this recipe with the note that she couldn't remember whether it was Sitto's or her friend Mary Maroon's. I knew that Sitto was very close to Mary in my youth and after making this, realized that it was how Sitto made her Dibis. I was so happy to have it, as I didn't make this while Sitto was alive. I've modernized it a bit in the preparation.

SITTO NAIMA'S TAMARIND SYRUP
DIBIS TAMAR HINDI MIN SITTO NAIMA

3	LBS. TAMARIND PODS (TAMAR HINDI)
6	LEMONS, JUICED
6	CUPS POMEGRANATE JUICE
6	CUPS SUGAR
1/8	TEASPOON LEMON SALT (SEE GLOSSARY)

Step 1: Place the tamarind pods into a large 4 qt. bowl and rinse a few times with cold water to remove any surface residue. Peel the shells and remove any loose fibers and rinse again. Cover the fruit with fresh, cold water and soak overnight.

Step 2: The next day, save the soaking water. Place the softened tamarind into a colander and place the colander back into the bowl. Use your fingers to squeeze the pods, crushing them to release the sticky paste. Gradually pour the soaking water over your fingers and through the seeds and fibers as you continue to squeeze in order to facilitate this process. Any remaining pulp will be eased through. Remove the colander and discard the stems, seeds and fibers.

Step 3: Place a fine strainer over another large bowl and spoon the pulp through the strainer, using a wooden spoon. You will have about 3 cups of pulp.

Step 4: Pour the strained pulp mixture into a large 6 qt. non-aluminum pot along with the lemon juice and heat to warm it. Remove from the heat and pour through a strainer which has been lined with cheesecloth and back into a clean bowl. This will remove any remaining particles of shell or tiny bits of seed and fiber.

Step 5: Rinse out the 6 qt. pot and return the strained mixture back into it. Add the pomegranate juice and heat to a boil. Then lower to a simmer, uncovered, for about 1 1/2 hours. Stir from time to time with a wooden spoon, not metal.

Then add the sugar and continue to simmer for another 4 to 5 hours until it darkens further. Taste for tartness and adjust if necessary during this simmer. Check your progress by placing a tablespoon of the syrup on a plate to let it cool. If it is the consistency of molasses, it is ready. During the last 30 minutes, add the lemon salt and stir in. Remove from the heat to let the mixture cool. Then pour the syrup into clean glass jars and store in a cool place for up to 18 months. There is no need to refrigerate this syrup. This yields about 4 to 5 cups.

Cook's Notes: I have used a food mill with a coarse disk and then a fine one instead of the colander and strainer and it has worked well.

The syrup tends to billow up when stirred towards the end of the simmer. Stir occasionally and with caution and keep the heat low to avoid a spillover. I have found that the syrup develops light brown bubbles on top when it's nearly finished.

I recommend a stovetop diffuser for such a long simmer. This prevents scorching of the pan and the heat will be evenly diffused and therefore will be more consistent.

I want to include my grandmother's good friend Aleya Sayegh's recipe. Her ratios and ingredients are a bit different and her tamarind source uses the peeled tamarind in a wet block form. This variety claims to be pitless but contains some pits and fibers.

ALEYA'S TAMARIND SYRUP
DIBIS TAMAR HINDI MIN ALEYA

10	14 OZ. PACKAGES OF WET TAMARIND BLOCK (TAMAR HINDI)
1	QT. WATER
4	CUPS SUGAR, OR MORE TO TASTE
10	LEMONS, JUICED

Step 1: Place the blocks of tamarind, which have been broken into small pieces, into a 6 to 8 qt. pot. Then add the water, cover with a lid and let soak overnight.

Step 2: Drain out the water and reserve. Place the tamarind into a colander. Rinse out the pot and place the colander over the same pot. Using a large wooden or plastic spoon or your hands, strain the solids through, pressing down on the tamarind, extracting the pulp through the colander. Pour the reserved water and some lemon juice to get the last remaining pulp through the colander, discarding any fibers, seeds or pieces that remain after straining. A food mill is another effective way of extracting pulp.

Step 3: Strain the pulp and liquids again but through a fine mesh strainer, which has been placed over a large bowl. This will yield about 3 cups of strained pulp.

Step 4: Rinse the pot and then add the pulp and liquids, sugar and lemon juice and bring to a boil over medium heat. Then lower the flame to a simmer, cover and cook for about 2 to 4 hours, stirring from time to time. This should thicken to a molasses consistency. Do not let it overflow or burn. Taste at mid-point to determine if more sugar or lemon is needed. The syrup should have a sweet/sour flavor.

Place in clean glass jars and store in a cool, dry place for 12 to 18 months.

Cook's Notes: Use a non-metal stirring spoon. Do not use an aluminum pot. I use a diffuser under the syrup to keep it from burning or sticking to the pot.

I've found that the supposed wet block with no pits does have a few stray pits and several fibers and pieces of seed. It is less tedious to work with than the actual pods, but I would not eliminate Steps 2 and 3 to ensure a smooth syrup.

Wet tamarind is available in Indian and Thai markets and online as well.

Through the years, I have been determined to find an easy way to prepare one of the most important ingredients in the cuisine of Aleppo, Syria. The Tamarind Syrup, an integral part of many Aleppo dishes, lends a unique sweet and sour tangy flavor. It's unlike any other condiment you've tried and is the identity of good Aleppian cooking.

And so, in my never-ending quest to make this important staple of the cook's pantry, I have tried to make a smaller batch of the Tamarind Syrup, with my grandmother's version as a guide. I did find that the wet blocks are easier to obtain and this batch did not take more than an hour of preparation. Hopefully, it will be practical to make this every few months.

TAMARIND SYRUP IV
DIBIS TAMAR HINDI ARB'A

7	**CUPS OF WATER**
2	**14 OZ. PACKAGES WET TAMARIND BLOCK WITH NO PITS (TAMAR HINDI)**
4	**CUPS POMEGRANATE JUICE**
6	**CUPS SUGAR**
1 1/4	**CUPS LEMON JUICE OR LEMON JUICE CONCENTRATE**
1/2	**TEASPOON LEMON SALT (SEE GLOSSARY)**

Boil the water and set aside.

Step 1: Place the blocks of tamarind in a colander and then place in a large 5 qt. pot or bowl. Break the blocks up into pieces. Then pour the boiled water over the broken blocks. Cover with a lid and let steep for 30 minutes.

Step 2: Take the colander out of the pot, pouring the water into a measuring cup with a pour spout. Then place the colander back into the pot and using a small amount of water at a time, pour over the tamarind pieces. As you pour, use a large wooden or plastic spoon to press down on the tamarind, extracting the pulp through the colander. Continue with the water, extracting and using your hands, if preferred, to squeeze out the pulp and water through the colander. The remaining fibers, seeds and pieces are to be discarded.

Step 3: Take the pulp/water and pour through a fine mesh strainer, which has been placed over another large bowl. It may be necessary to once again pour this pulp mixture through cheesecloth, if you still see specs of seeds or fibers. This yields 4 to 5 cups of the strained pulp.

Step 4: Pour the pulp into a 6 qt. pot. Add the pomegranate juice, sugar, lemon juice and lemon salt and cook over medium to high heat until the mixture boils. Lower the heat to a simmer and cook, uncovered, for about 4 hours, stirring from time to time. Taste at mid-point to adjust the lemon to sugar ratio. The mixture should have a tangy, sweet/sour taste. The mixture will have a topping of light brown foam towards the end of the simmer. It will thicken to a molasses consistency. As it thickens, be careful in stirring it, since it will tend to billow up. Do not let it overflow or burn.

Allow it to cool to room temperature and pour into clean glass jars. This makes about 5 1/2 cups. Store in a cool, dry place for 12 to 18 months.

Cook's Notes: Use a non-metal stirring spoon. Do not use an aluminum pot.

I have found that the supposed pitless wet block does have a few stray pits and several fibers and pieces of seed. Although it is less tedious to work with than the actual pods, I would not eliminate Step 3.
Wet tamarind is available on-line and at Indian and Thai markets.

In the previous recipes, I've prepared this syrup using the fresh pods and the wet tamarind blocks. Now as a final alternative, I have prepared it using pure tamarind concentrate. I'd hoped that the strained commercially prepared paste would produce a similar product. Much to my delight, this is a more convenient version and in a smaller quantity. Although it's not as authentic in taste as the fresh pods, even a novice cook can try this version without much effort.

TAMARIND SYRUP V
DIBIS TAMAR HINDI KHAMSI

1	16 OZ. JAR TAMARIND CONCENTRATE PASTE (OR 2 – 8 OZ. JARS)
6	CUPS WATER
1	CUP LEMON JUICE OR LEMON JUICE CONCENTRATE
1	48 OZ. JAR POMEGRANATE JUICE
8	CUPS SUGAR
1/4	TEASPOON LEMON SALT (SEE GLOSSARY)

Heat the tamarind concentrate with the water, lemon and pomegranate juice in a 6 qt. pot. Bring to a boil and immediately lower to a simmer, uncovered, for 1 hour.

Add the sugar and stir well. Continue to simmer, uncovered, until the mixture becomes darker and syrupy, about 4 to 5 hours. Taste at a mid-point to adjust for sugar or lemon to taste. The ideal syrup will be sweet/sour and tangy. In the last half-hour, add the lemon salt. Test a few tablespoons in a small bowl to cool to determine if it is the consistency of molasses. Towards the end of the simmer, the syrup will take on lighter brown foam on top and will billow when stirred. This is another tip that the syrup has thickened and is near completion.

The cooled syrup is now ready to place in clean glass jars. This makes about 7 1/2 cups. Store in a cool, dry place for 12 to 18 months.

Cook's Notes: Use a non-metal stirring spoon. Do not use an aluminum pot. I use a diffuser under the pot when simmering to avoid any possibility of burning the syrup.

Tamarind concentrate is readily available from Middle Eastern, Asian and Mexican markets, Amazon and other online stores.

Tamarind Syrup

Fresh White Cheese and Syrian String Cheese

Sitto's cool cellar, with its brine jars filled with homemade cheese and preserved grapevine leaves was a delicious place to explore for this young girl.

Syrian String Cheese

Homemade string cheese is so easy and fun... the challenge is finding the raw cheese curd for melting and braiding, which is available at Middle Eastern stores. Today, some markets are offering the packaged braided cheese, known as Syrian or Armenian string cheese. However, nothing compares in flavor to the real thing. Sitto served this as a Mezze dish, as a satisfying sandwich on Syrian Bread or as a quick morning breakfast. And I always remember it on our picnics with the strands unwound, alongside fresh baby cucumbers, radishes and Jersey garden tomatoes on a hot day.

SYRIAN STRING CHEESE
JIBNEH IMSAYECHAH

12	LBS. WHOLE MILK CHEESE CURD OR MOZZARELLA CURD
1	TABLESPOON GROUND BLACK CHERRY KERNELS (MAHLAB) (SEE GLOSSARY)
1/4	CUP NIGELLA SEEDS, CLEANED AND RINSED (SEE GLOSSARY)

Prepare a brine solution using this basic ratio:

1	TABLESPOON SALT
1	CUP WATER

Cut the cheese into 1" cubes.

Have a small bowl of ice water nearby to cool your fingers when needed.

Pour about 1/2 cup of water into a large 10" to 12" sauté pan (not Teflon) and boil. Lower to medium heat and then place about 1 cup of cubed cheese into the pan. Keep turning and flattening the cheese until melted using a wooden spoon. Make sure the cheese is evenly melted into a ball. Do not overheat, as this will turn the cheese into a liquid.

Remove the hot melted lump of cheese onto a dish, sprinkle quickly with a pinch of Mahlab and some black nigella seeds. Pat into a ball and separate the center with your thumb to make a center hole. From this (and this is the fun part, once you get the hang of it), pull the cheese into strings, stretching and bouncing the strings as you pull. Continue to pull, rewrapping as you double and triple the strings, working quickly before the cheese cools. Twist into a braidlike shape and tie the ends into itself, making a figure eight with the strands. You will improve as you practice with this one. If you have ever purchased the commercial braided cheese, you know how it is twisted and braided into the shape of an 8.

Put the braid into the prepared brine solution for only 1 hour before removing from the brine and wrapping in plastic bags for refrigeration or freezing.

Cook's Notes: The liquid in the sauté pan turns milky white after making 3 or 4 cheese braids. Pour these cheese drippings into a container to save for making Kahek (See the recipe in Breakfast) and start again with a fresh 1/2 cup of water boiled in the fry pan. Add more cheese to continue the process until all the cheese is melted and braided.

My grandmother kept a bowl of cold water nearby to dip her fingers into because the cheese is hot. The brine solution basic ratio is to be increased, depending upon the amount of cheese made.

Whole fresh Mozzarella (not salted) can be used as a replacement for either of the curd cheeses. Cut into cubes and proceed with the recipe.

I should mention that the homemade version is worlds better because of the use of Mahlab and nigella seeds. It's the real thing and the traditional way of preparing this cheese.

Yogurt Cheese can be a good staple in the refrigerator for breakfast, snacks or as an appetizer for Mezze. Having it on hand and then adding your own touches will allow for quick and healthy dishes for the family.

BASIC YOGURT CHEESE
LABNEH

1	QT. WHOLE MILK YOGURT (PLAIN) HOMEMADE OR COMMERCIAL
1/4	TEASPOON SALT

Mix the salt into the yogurt and set aside.

Prepare a 2 qt. bowl by placing a doubled strip of cheesecloth, about 24" long, into the bowl and up over the rim. Repeat another doubled strip across it, forming an X at the bottom of the bowl.

Spoon the yogurt into the cheesecloth and tie the four corners of the cloth around a long-handled spoon and knot it. Then place the spoon over the top of the bowl, leaving the yogurt sack to hang inside the bowl. Then put the bowl into the refrigerator to drain overnight or for as much as 24 hours. The cheese will get firmer as it drains.

Check for liquid in the bottom of the bowl and drain it from time to time during this period.

The next day, squeeze out any remaining liquid in the cheesecloth and discard the water that has accumulated. The yogurt cheese will be firm, but creamy. Place the yogurt cheese into a smaller bowl with a lid. Chill. To serve plain, spread the yogurt cheese onto pita bread quarters. This recipe makes about 2 cups plain yogurt cheese.

Cook's Notes: Each yogurt produces a slightly different taste. I have used homemade yogurt and a few brands of commercial plain, low fat yogurt. The result is always creamy, but the amount of water draining from the yogurt varies. I prefer keeping the cheese draining for at least 24 hours or more. I also noted that the tanginess differed both with the time it drains and with the homemade or commercial brands.

For a sweetened version:

2	TABLESPOONS SUPERFINE OR CONFECTIONERS SUGAR – TO TASTE
1/2	TEASPOON CINNAMON, OPTIONAL

In a small cup, blend the sugar and cinnamon, mix the sugar and cinnamon into the cheese, gradually, and adjust to taste.

Cook's Notes: I have also stuffed dates with plain or sweetened yogurt cheese or spread the yogurt cheese onto dried apricots. Like my grandmother, I have found these to be a tasty breakfast alternative.

For a savory version:

1	TABLESPOON EXTRA VIRGIN OLIVE OIL
	DASH SALT - TO TASTE
1	CLOVE GARLIC, CRUSHED (OPTIONAL)
1	TEASPOON CHOPPED FRESH MINT
1/2	TEASPOON CHOPPED FRESH PARSLEY

In a 2 qt. bowl, mix the oil, salt, garlic and herbs into the yogurt cheese and chill.

Serve as a spread for pita bread, crackers, vegetables or flatbread.

Cook's Notes: The oil content can also be varied. Some prefer less oil. In any case, when adding herbs and spices, some oil will be needed.

To make this spread your own, use any other of your favorite herbs, such as fresh thyme, dill, oregano, basil or rosemary.

Another option would be to sprinkle the cheese with Zahtar spice (See Glossary) instead of the herbs. When I have a wish for our Syrian string cheese, I found that I can mix the plain yogurt cheese with 1/4 teaspoon ground Mahlab and 1/2 teaspoon of nigella seeds. Although it has a different texture than the string cheese, the taste is similar and delicious.

Savory Yogurt Cheese

In some Syrian cities, as well as in other regions of the Levant, sweet and tart Pomegranate Syrup is preferred over Tamarind Syrup. It is used as a condiment and flavoring in the preparation of many Middle Eastern dishes and is considered a basic for many cooks. For this reason, I've decided to add this homemade version of the syrup to the cookbook.

POMEGRANATE SYRUP
DIBIS RIMAN

4	**CUPS POMEGRANATE JUICE, UNSWEETENED**
2	**CUPS SUGAR, OR TO TASTE**
1/2	**CUP LEMON JUICE, FRESH SQUEEZED**
	DASH LEMON SALT

Dissolve the sugar and lemon juice in the pomegranate juice and bring to a boil in a 5 qt. pot. Lower to a simmer, uncovered, for about 50 minutes or until thickened to a syrup consistency.

At a mid point, check the sugar content and add more, if preferred.

The simmer time can vary depending on the thickness of the syrup desired. Keep in mind that the syrup will thicken more when cooled. Test the consistency by pouring a drop onto a plate and letting it cool. If it resembles a syrup, it is ready.

In the last few minutes of the simmer, add the dash of lemon salt.

Remove from the heat and allow to cool somewhat before pouring into clean, sterile glass jars. Store in a cool area or the refrigerator. Makes 2 to 3 cups.

Cook's Notes: This syrup may be added as a flavoring or condiment in place of tamarind syrup, if preferred.

Dessert Topping: To use as a delicious topping for ice cream, waffles or other baked goods, eliminate the lemon juice from the recipe and proceed as above. As a drink, add a bit of this sweeter syrup to a glass, filling the rest with water and ice.

Lemon salt, also known as citric acid, is available in Middle Eastern markets and on-line through spice merchants.

AN ALEPPO BREAKFAST

I have fond memories of special breakfasts when Sitto would prepare Mamunea before we awoke. This versatile breakfast dish was served warm with Syrian bread for dipping. There are other delicious variations of this as a rich oven-baked dessert or as a wonderful filling for Aros turnovers. These recipes are all included in this section and in Sweets. In any case, my grandchildren love this and it is their first request when we are together!

BREAKFAST FARINA
MAMUNEA

1	QT. MILK
3/4	CUP SUGAR, OR TO TASTE
1/4	LB. MARGARINE
3/4	CUP SEMOLINA (SMEDE) OR FARINA (NOT QUICK-COOKING)
	CINNAMON FOR GARNISH

Pour the milk and sugar into a large 5 qt. pot over medium heat, being careful not to boil or scald the milk.

While the milk and sugar are heating, melt the margarine or butter in a large 12" skillet until melted. Add the semolina or farina, stirring constantly to distribute the butter evenly to prevent burning and allow to brown to the color of wet sand. This will enhance the flavor.

When the milk begins to simmer, gradually add the semolina mixture by large spoonfuls, stirring completely in order to prevent lumps from forming. When all the semolina has been added and the mixture is well blended, cover the pot and turn off the heat.

Stir every 3 minutes until the pudding is very thick. This will be approximately 6 to 9 or more minutes. The Mamunea is as thick as cooked oatmeal. Pour into bowls while still warm, sprinkle with cinnamon and serve with warm pita bread quarters.

Any remaining portion may be refrigerated and re-heated by microwaving for a minute or two before serving.

Breakfast Farina

Sitto's Kahek

I fondly remember Sitto's Kahek as crunchy biscuit rings, flavored with fennel seed, anise, black nigella seeds and Mahlab, all the typical Aleppo spices. These biscuits were a good start to the day along with Syrian cheese and fruit. I loved finding them in her favorite pot in the pantry. It was a great treat as an after-school snack and later, as a grown-up, I enjoyed them with a cup of coffee or tea. Sitto loved these and made them often. This is her recipe.

SITTO NAIMA'S BREAKFAST BISCUITS
KAHEK MIN SITTO NAIMA

6	CUPS SEMOLINA (SMEDE)
6	CUPS FLOUR
2	TABLESPOONS SUGAR
1	TABLESPOON BAKING POWDER
1/2	TEASPOON SALT
1	TABLESPOON FENNEL SEED, GROUND
1	TABLESPOON ANISE SEEDS, WHOLE
1 - 1 1/2	TABLESPOONS NIGELLA SEEDS (SEE GLOSSARY)
1	CUP WARM WATER
1	PKG. DRY YEAST
1	TEASPOON GROUND BLACK CHERRY KERNELS (MAHLAB) (SEE GLOSSARY)
1	LB. CRISCO, MELTED
1/2	LB. MARGARINE, MELTED
2	CUPS CHEESE DRIPPINGS (PAGE 16) OR WARM WATER

Mix the dry ingredients and spices in a large 8 to 10 qt. pot.

In a measuring cup: Mix the warm water and yeast together and set aside for 5 minutes. Add the ground black cherry kernels (Mahlab) and pour into the dry ingredients and mix.

Add the melted shortening to the dry ingredients. Then add the warm cheese drippings or warm water. Knead to a spongy consistency. Cover and let rise one hour in a warm, draft-free place.

Preheat the oven to 325 degrees. Break the dough into walnut-sized balls, cover and let rest for 15 minutes.

Take each ball and roll into a thin cigar shape about 6" long. Then form a bracelet, overlapping the ends to seal. Keep any unbaked dough balls covered until they are rolled and baked.

Place the biscuits on an ungreased baking sheet about 1" apart. Bake for 30 minutes until the tops and bottoms are golden.

Remove the biscuits, cool completely and place into a sealed container to store until serving. Makes approximately 96 biscuits.

Cook's Notes: A longer baking time will produce a crunchy biscuit, which is the original recipe. Since ovens vary, you may prefer to lower the heat to 300 degrees if the biscuits are browning too much within this baking time. After baking, you may also leave the biscuits in the oven as it cools for an even crisper finish.

For the best flavor, I use my spice grinder to crush the whole Mahlab and the fennel seeds, as needed.

If using the cheese drippings making string cheese, (See Basics) it may already contain the nigella seeds. If so, add no more or very little.

I have successfully frozen baked Kahek in a sealed plastic container enclosed in a plastic baggy in order to avoid freezer burn. Thaw at room temperature.

Warm in an oven to recapture that first-baked taste. I have successfully cut this recipe in half.

Sitto Naima's Breakfast Biscuits and Syrian String Cheese

Here's a note to every baker who thought that a recipe needed a little something, along with apologies to Sitto. I decided to try her Kahek with clarified butter instead of the Crisco/margarine mixture. I increased the spices, which I love, and eliminated the baking powder. It made for a crunchier biscuit and the family loved the result! If you try this, I hope you like it as well!

AUTHOR'S BREAKFAST BISCUITS
KAHEK MU' ALLIF

2 1/2	**CUPS SEMOLINA (SMEDE)**
3	**CUPS FLOUR**
1	**TABLESPOON SUGAR**
1/4	**TEASPOON SALT**
1	**TABLESPOON GROUND FENNEL SEED**
1	**TABLESPOON ANISE SEEDS, WHOLE**
1	**TABLESPOON NIGELLA SEEDS, OR TO TASTE (SEE GLOSSARY)**
1	**CUP WARM WATER**
1	**PKG. DRY YEAST**
1	**TABLESPOON GROUND BLACK CHERRY KERNELS (MAHLAB) (SEE GLOSSARY)**
1 1/2	**CUPS CLARIFIED BUTTER, MELTED (PAGE 7)**
1	**CUP CHEESE DRIPPINGS (PAGE 16) OR WARM WATER**

Using these ingredients, proceed with Sitto's Breakfast Biscuits, Kahek, per recipe instructions on page 24.

Cook's Notes: I split Sitto's recipe in half, as many of today's bakers prefer trying a recipe in a smaller quantity to see if they like it. In Sitto's day, lots of family around made it simpler to bake pounds of these Kahek!

See other Cook's Notes in Sitto's Kahek recipe before proceeding.

Author's Breakfast Biscuits

Date Biscuits

My husband's Aunt Lizzie Atieh made her Kahek in a much richer fashion. I'm reminded again that the later generations had more access to ingredients in America that the late 19th century Syrians did not. Also, the poorer people, using community ovens, had a simpler and humbler way of cooking. We loved this version on my husband's side of the family. These richer biscuits are more like buttery, decadent cookies. They are marvelous filled with dates and flavored with the drippings of homemade string cheese. When made in a few steps, these delightful treats are relatively easy.

AUNT LIZZIE'S DATE BISCUITS
KAHEK B' AJWEH MIN AMAMI LIZZIE

Date Filling:

2	LBS. MEDJOOL DATES
4	TABLESPOONS BUTTER OR MARGARINE
1 1/2	TEASPOONS ORANGE BLOSSOM WATER (*MAHZAHAD*)

Rinse the dates in a medium saucepan and add enough water to cover. Bring to a boil and remove from the heat to allow them to cool. When cooled, remove skins and pits and place in a 3 qt. bowl. Squeeze in the butter by hand to mix throughout. Add the Orange Blossom Water to blend in and impart its flavoring. Refrigerate and then prepare the dough.

Dough:

1	**PACKAGE DRY YEAST**
	PINCH SUGAR
1/2	**CUP WARM WATER**
1	**LB. MARGARINE**
1	**CUP CRISCO SHORTENING**
8	**CUPS SEMOLINA (SMEDE)**
3	**CUPS FLOUR**
1 1/2	**TABLESPOONS GROUND BLACK CHERRY KERNELS (MAHLAB) (SEE GLOSSARY)**
1 1/2	**CUPS STRING CHEESE DRIPPINGS (PAGE 16) OR WATER, WARMED**
1/4	**CUP NIGELLA SEEDS (MORE OR LESS, AS PREFERRED)**

In a measuring cup, mix the yeast, sugar and water, set aside for 5 minutes.

In a microwave: Melt the margarine and Crisco together in a 2 qt. glass bowl. Set aside to cool somewhat. In a

large 5 or 6 qt. pot, mix the semolina and flour together to blend.

Mix the ground Mahlab into the warm cheese drippings or water.

Pour the yeast/water mixture into the flour mixture and stir in to begin to form a dough.

Add the cheese drippings into the dough and work in with your hands as you gradually sprinkle in the nigella seeds, incorporating as much or as little as you prefer.

Gradually add the melted margarine/Crisco to the dough and knead for about 5 to 7 minutes until the shortening is well incorporated. The dough will feel greasy but will bake into the Kahek.

Cover the dough and put it into a warm place to let rise for two hours. Remove the dates from the refrigerator.

Preheat the oven to 450 degrees.

Take a small ball of dough, about 1 1/4" diameter and flatten into a circle. Add the date mixture, shaped about the size of a pinky finger, to the center of the dough circle. Roll the dough away from you into the same finger shape, with the seam-side down. Then curve the ends of the dough, gently sealing and bending the ends to form a crescent.

Place on an ungreased baking sheet, away from the edges of the pan. They may be placed 1" apart, as they do not rise much. They will bake to about a 3" crescent.

Place on the middle rack of the oven and bake for 5 minutes, switching to the top rack at the halfway point and bake for another 5 or 6 minutes. Check to make sure they do not brown but stay a light golden color.

Cool on a wire rack and then keep in an airtight container at room temperature.

Cook's Notes: This recipe produces a softer, richer version of Kahek, more like a filled shortbread-type biscuit, with a grainier texture from the semolina. Although the dough is not sweetened, the date filling provides just enough of a sweet taste for a breakfast or light dessert. This is wonderful with Arab coffee (on page 168).

I have also used homemade Apricot Orange Marmalade (on page 29) as an alternate filling for those who are not "date" fans. If using, add a teaspoon of marmalade or any favorite jam to the center of the circle of dough and roll as above.

Many mornings, Sitto's breakfast would consist of sliced white cheese on Syrian bread, which we called Khubiz, along with some fresh fruit or olives. She loved this cheese, which she called Jibneh Khadra. It literally means fresh cheese. I always remember those white globes of cheese in her refrigerator. I liked this homemade cheese then, but I really love it now for breakfast or sliced as an appetizer with olives, crackers or flatbread.

FRESH WHITE SYRIAN CHEESE
JIBNEH KHADRA

1/2	GALLON WHOLE MILK
2	RENNET TABLETS (JUNKET BRAND OR OTHER)
1	TEASPOON KOSHER SALT, OR MORE TO TASTE

Fresh White Syrian Cheese

Heat the milk in a large 5 qt. pot over medium heat until warm but not hot. Do not allow to boil, as this will not work. If you have a thermometer, heat to 96 degrees or when you can put your finger into the milk comfortably. Keep the burner on the lowest setting to keep the milk warm.

Break up the rennet tablets and stir into the warm milk with a plastic or wooden spoon to dissolve and blend well. Cover and leave for 30 minutes. Then stir again, cover and keep on the lowest heat for 1 hour.

Turn off the heat and keep covered and undisturbed for up to 4 hours. If it's ready, you'll note that the mixture will now appear yellow and watery on top. If you test the bottom with a spoon, you'll see that the cheese solids may be beginning to form into what look like pieces of cottage cheese.

Prepare a colander by placing it into a deep bowl. Line the bottom of the colander with two long strips of double layer cheesecloth forming an X.

Use a slotted spoon to scoop the cheese curds out of the liquid and into the cheesecloth-covered colander. Take the four ends of the cheesecloth and squeeze the cheese to drain as much of the liquid out of it as possible. Open the cheesecloth and sprinkle the salt over the cheese. Taste it and add more salt if needed. Knot the four ends of the cheesecloth over a large wooden spoon and hang this over a deep bowl. Refrigerate for a few hours.

Wrap the cheese in new cheesecloth or paper toweling. Place the ball of cheese into a smaller plastic or stainless steel strainer. Add a bowl under the strainer to catch any more drippings. Place a small dish over the wrapped cheese to weigh it down. You may need to change the paper toweling for a day or so as the moisture is released from the cheese and it becomes firmer. Refrigerate until the cheese is firm and can be sliced.

Cook's Notes: Rennet, in tablet form and sometimes as a liquid, is produced from the stomach of a calf. Vegetarian versions are also available. See "Where To Buy It (Redco Foods)" for more information.

I remember my grandmother taking out some marvelous old pieces brought from Syria to serve her guests. I especially recall a beautiful silver and burgundy glass bowl with tiny forks attached for picking up pieces of candied apricot, called Turkish delight or her freshly-stuffed dates.

The Middle East was plentiful with apricots, dates and figs and Sitto grew up loving these healthy sweets. I remember, in her later years, she would be absolutely delighted with a tray of dried fruit. This wonderful marmalade is a frequent breakfast topper to warmed Syrian bread.

APRICOT ORANGE MARMALADE
MIRABBA MISHMOSH MA'BURDQAN

1	**CUP DRIED APRICOTS, DICED**
1/2	**CUP COLD WATER**
1/2	**CUP ORANGE JUICE**
1/3	**CUP SUGAR**, MORE OR LESS TO TASTE

Place the apricots into a small bowl with the cold water to cover and soak for a few hours.

Pour into a 3 qt. saucepan. Add the juice and sugar and bring to a boil. Lower to a simmer for just 15 minutes.

Towards the end of the simmer, mash the apricots with a hand blender or potato masher. Do not puree but leave them with some texture. Check the sugar content and add more, if desired. Continue to simmer for the remaining minutes until soft and thickened.

Place into a clean, sterile jar and refrigerate. Serve over Syrian bread for breakfast, or a snack. This recipe makes one cup.

Cook's Notes: In mashing the apricots, I prefer a chunkier version, so I do not mash them very much. During cooking, they may have softened and broken down enough to eliminate this step.

I prefer a less sweet marmalade, but you may prefer more sugar. If so, feel free to add more.

Apricot Orange Marmalade

Apricot Pastry Turnovers

APRICOT PASTRY TURNOVERS
SAMBUSAK MA' MISHMOSH

Dough:

1/4	**LB. BUTTER OR MARGARINE**
3	**TABLESPOONS SUGAR**
1	**EGG, BEATEN**
1 1/3	**CUPS FLOUR**
1	**TEASPOON BAKING POWDER**

In a small 1 qt. bowl, combine the butter and sugar until blended. Then add the egg.

In a medium 2 qt. bowl, blend the flour with the baking powder and add the butter mixture to it to make a soft ball. Wrap in wax paper and chill for 30 minutes.

Filling:

1	**CUP SWEETENED YOGURT CHEESE, PAGE 17**
1/2	**CUP APRICOT ORANGE MARMALADE, PAGE 29, OR ANY FAVORITE JAM**

Preheat the oven to 400 degrees.

Roll the dough out between layers of wax paper, to 1/8" thick. Using a 3" biscuit cutter or a glass, cut rounds in the dough. Place the rounds on an ungreased baking sheet.

Place 1 teaspoon of the yogurt cheese on each round. Top the cheese with 1 teaspoon of the marmalade. Close the round to form a turnover. With the tines of a fork or with your fingers, seal the edges.

Bake the pastries for 8 to 10 minutes. Serve warm or cool and place in a covered container. Store in the refrigerator until ready to serve. Warm the turnovers before serving.

Cook's Notes: I have used the yogurt cheese sweetened or unsweetened.

Sitto would often give me a tasty breakfast or snack, which she called Dibis W' Tahina. Making a quick sandwich of Syrian bread, my grandmother would top it with Tahini and then the Date syrup. I really loved this and at the time, didn't realize how good it was for me. In the Middle East, this is often a simple breakfast.

TAHINI AND DATE SYRUP SANDWICHES
DIBIS W' TAHINA

1/4	CUP TAHINI
1/4	CUP DATE SYRUP (DIBIS)
	SESAME SEEDS, OPTIONAL
	PITA BREAD

To prepare the date syrup:

2	LBS. PITTED MEDJOOL DATES
	WATER

Cut the dates in half, ensuring there are no pit pieces.

Rinse the dates and place in a large 4 qt. bowl, with enough water to cover. Cover with plastic wrap and soak overnight.

Puree the dates and liquid in a food processor.

Pour into a medium 3 qt. saucepan and stir. Heat the mixture and then lower to a simmer for about 1 hour, or until it thickens to a syrup.

Tahini and Date Syrup Sandwiches

Cool and place in a clean jar. Store opened jars in the refrigerator. This will yield about 1 cup.

To prepare the sandwich:
Spread the tahini over the halved pita bread. Top with the date syrup. A sprinkling of sesame seeds may also be added.

Cook's Notes: Dibis, a staple in the Middle East, may be either date or carob syrup, depending on the region. Date syrup is a good replacement for molasses in recipes. Use it over yogurt cheese or in yogurt, as well as into dressings or meat marinades.

Honey may be substituted for the date syrup as another option.

My sister Elaine and I would sneak into Sitto's pantry to peek into the pot that she always kept filled with baked treats. Her pantry, which was actually a room under the stairs that stayed cool all year round, was a perfect place to "treasure hunt." We always knew which pastries were date-filled and which had our favorite farina (Mamunea) filling. We always opted for the farina pockets first. I think the date filling is a more "grown-up" kind of taste, unusual with its hint of flora...it has a bit of Orange Blossom Water, Mahzahad, mixed with the dates.

Sitto was the only woman in our circle who made this wonderful turnover. In fact, many didn't even know how it was made. It's still a wonder today how we managed to keep this recipe in the family. My mother tells me that Sitto's mother-in-law, Sitto Lucy, taught her everything she knew about cooking. She had lived with her in-laws after marrying Giddo Bashir and that this was probably her recipe. Family and guests usually needed no convincing to try these turnovers for breakfast or for an unusual dessert after a light meal. All of us love them, but I have to smile when my grandchildren ask me to "please make those Mamunea pockets!"

These soft as a cloud and addictive turnovers are fragrant with a unique Middle Eastern spice called Mahlab. There were three ways to make this wonderful sweet bread, as plain rounds, with farina filling called Aros or with a date filling called Kateh and that recipe follows.

This recipe is always made ahead and then enjoyed for breakfast, for snacks or dessert. Even with today's appliances, I split this recipe into two steps. I make the filling and clarified butter on one day and the turnovers on the next.

I should mention my youthful mistake when first making these delicacies in my Illinois kitchen. After getting verbal instructions by phone from my grandmother, I mixed the Mahlab into the dough. Much to my surprise, the little round spice pebbles didn't melt. After frantically calling my grandmother about this, she laughed and told me I needed to grind the spice in a mortar and pestle or as I later discovered, my blender, before adding the powdered spice to my dough. I then realized that long-distance directions are flawed! Now that I'm older and have cooked for the last 45 years, my experience will sometimes allow me to forget that the younger cook may not have the necessary background information. And so I've considered this in recording and perfecting these recipes. In any case, young cooks, these are worth the effort!

I use my grandmother's hand-carved pastry block to imprint the top of the Aros with a beautiful floral design. I also have her round wood edge tool with serrated edges for finishing the border of the turnover and sealing. I treasure these old pieces and think of all the loving hands of my ancestors who baked while using these worn implements.

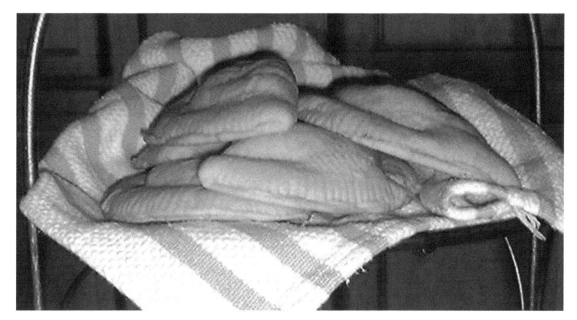

Sitto's Aleppo Turnovers

SITTO'S ALEPPO TURNOVERS
AROS HALABY MIN SITTO

8	CUPS SEMOLINA (SMEDE)
4	CUPS FLOUR (ADD 1 CUP MORE FOR LIGHTER TURNOVERS)
1	CUP SUGAR
2	PACKAGES DRY YEAST
2	CUPS WARM WATER (DIVIDED USE)
2	CUPS MILK
2	TABLESPOONS GROUND BLACK CHERRY KERNELS (MAHLAB) (SEE GLOSSARY)
2 1/4	CUPS CLARIFIED BUTTER, WARMED, BASICS, PAGE 7

In a large 6 to 8 qt. pot, mix the semolina, flour and sugar until well blended.

Mix the yeast packets in 1 cup of warm water until dissolved. Set aside for 5 minutes.

Heat the milk in a 1 qt. saucepan or microwave until warm but not hot and add the finely ground Mahlab and stir.

Add the dissolved yeast to the dry ingredients and mix with your hands. Slowly add the warm milk mixture and then knead. Add the other cup of warm water and continue kneading until the mixture starts to stick together and appears "spongy."

Begin to add the warmed butter to the dough, but very gradually, while continuing to knead for another 10 to 15 minutes. The dough will begin to get soft and plump as all the butter is absorbed. Cover the dough and place in a draft-free spot, like a cold oven. Let rise for about 1 1/2 hours until doubled in bulk.

If the filling has not been prepared ahead, use this time to proceed with this filling recipe below, per the instructions in Breakfast Farina (on page 22). Then pour the mixture into a rectangular glass pan. Sprinkle with cinnamon, cool, cover and refrigerate until ready to fill the turnovers before baking.
Farina Filling (Mamunea) for Aleppo Turnovers:

2	QTS. MILK
1 3/4	CUPS SUGAR
1/2	LB. MARGARINE OR CLARIFIED BUTTER
2	CUPS FARINA
	CINNAMON FOR GARNISH

Imprinting Turnovers

Making Turnovers

Sitto's Aleppo Turnovers Unbaked

Sitto's Aleppo Turnovers With Farina Filling, Baked

Preparing the Aros: Preheat the oven to 400 degrees.

When the dough has risen, take a 2" diameter-size ball of dough and place on a baking cloth or a long piece of wax paper. Separate the rest of the dough in this same way and let all the dough balls rest, covered with a clean kitchen towel or cloth for 15 to 30 minutes.

Flatten a dough ball to about 6" diameter with a small pastry roller or your fingers. Make an imprint on one-half of the dough round. (See Cook's Notes) Then turn it over and put 2 to 3 heaping tablespoons of the Farina filling in the middle. Turn half of the dough circle over to form a turnover, keeping the imprinted side up.

Seal the edges with the crimping tool or the tines of a fork. Then pierce the top a few times with the fork. Place the turnovers on ungreased, insulated or heavy cookie sheets. Thin sheets will brown the bottoms too quickly. Bake the turnovers approximately 10 minutes, depending on your oven. The bottom should be golden and the top should be light and only slightly tinged. Remove to cool on wire racks.

The turnovers are best served warm. If reheating, warm in a 350 degree oven. Do not microwave. This recipe makes approximately 45 to 50 turnovers, depending on the size.

Cook's Notes: Traditionally, the top center was imprinted with a hand-carved wooden block, much like a printer's block. This block has a floral motif. The carving would leave an imprint in the top, which baked up nicely and gave the turnovers a rich textural look. I still have my grandmother's decoratively carved block and love using it. Any wood block or clean stamp will work just fine. Or leave the top plain, if necessary or more convenient. (See the photo of the tools used.)

I should mention that plain, unfilled dough rounds with imprinted, pierced tops and with edges crimped all around were also made along with the filled turnovers. I now think it was because it's practically impossible to have the filling and the dough equal out every time; although in time, it's easier to judge. The plain round Aros are a less sweet, simpler breakfast bun.

I usually make the filling the day before I plan to bake the turnovers. I know this is not something that would be made before breakfast, but keeping the frozen turnovers for breakfast or snacks is something my family relies upon. They can be heated frozen, but it will take longer to warm them.

I freeze the cooled turnovers, four to a plastic freezer bag, in these proportions. This makes it much easier to remove a few at a time. This is my family's absolutely favorite breakfast pastry. They go like "hotcakes" so they will not be in your freezer very long!

My grandmother favored these date-filled turnovers, Kateh, and always made them along with the farina-filled pastries she called Aros. The fragrant date filling was a memorable taste of "home" to her.

ALEPPO TURNOVERS WITH DATE FILLING
KATEH HALABY MA' AJWEH

1	RECIPE PREPARED ALEPPO TURNOVER DOUGH (AROS) PAGE 33
2	16 OZ. PACKAGES MEDJOOL DATES
1/3	CUP SWEET BUTTER, ROOM TEMPERATURE
1	TEASPOON ORANGE BLOSSOM WATER (MAHZAHAD), OR LESS TO TASTE

Rinse the dates in a medium saucepan and add enough water to cover. Bring to a boil and remove from the heat to allow them to cool. When cooled, remove the skins and pits and place in a 3 qt. bowl. Add the butter to the dates and squeeze by hand to mix throughout. Add the Orange Blossom Water to blend in and impart its flavoring.

Roll the date mixture into 2" diameter balls and place on a sheet of wax paper. Flatten each date ball into a patty to be inserted into each turnover. Set aside.

Preheat the oven to 400 degrees.

Preparing the turnovers: When the dough has risen, take a 2" diameter-size ball of dough and place on a baking cloth or a long piece of wax paper. Separate the rest of the dough in this same way and let all the dough balls rest, covered with a clean kitchen towel or cloth for 15 to 30 minutes.

To make the turnovers: Flatten each dough ball to about 6" diameter with a small pastry or pizza roller or your fingers. Make an imprint on one half of the dough round. (See Cook's Notes.) Then turn it over and put the date patty in the middle. Turn half of the dough circle over to form a turnover, keeping the imprinted side up.
Seal the edges with the crimping roller or the tines of a fork. Then pierce the top a few times with the fork. Place the turnovers on heavy cookie sheets or insulated ones. Thin sheets will brown the bottoms too quickly. Bake the turnovers from 10 to 11 minutes, depending on your oven. The bottom should be golden and the top should be light and only slightly tinged.

Aleppo Turnovers with Date Filling

Remove to cool on wire racks and store in the refrigerator or freezer. This recipe makes about 40 to 50 turnovers, depending on the size.

They are best served warm, so a reheating for a few minutes in a 350 degree oven, until the filling is warm, will suffice. Do not microwave.

Cook's Notes: See the notes in the previous Aros recipe.

This date filling is used in several Aleppian pastries. Medjool dates are preferred, but other quality dates may be used for this filling. It's also possible to make a batch of these turnovers consisting of half date-filled and half farina-filled. In time, that may be your favorite way to make these!

APPETIZERS

I remember eating Hummus as a child, long before it became the fashionable healthy dip it is today. It was served as a side dish at home and was a big favorite as a Mezze dish at our church festivals. I remember a shiny layer of olive oil on top of this wonderful garlicky paste as we scooped it up with wedges of Syrian bread.

CHICKPEA DIP
HUMMUS B'TAHINA

1	15 OZ. CAN CHICKPEAS (GARBANZO BEANS)
6	TEASPOONS TAHINI
2	CLOVES GARLIC, PRESSED OR CRUSHED
1/2	LEMON, SQUEEZED
1/2	TEASPOON SALT
1	TEASPOON GROUND CUMIN
1/8	CUP OLIVE OIL
	DASH ALEPPO PEPPER OR PAPRIKA FOR GARNISH
	FRESH CHOPPED PARSLEY FOR GARNISH
	OLIVE OIL, DRIZZLED, FOR GARNISH

Drain the beans, saving the liquid. Rinse the beans and remove any skins.

In a blender or food processor, place the beans, tahini, garlic, lemon, salt, cumin and oil and process until smooth. Add some or all of the bean liquid until it becomes a paste suitable for dipping. This is also where you would adjust the spices according to taste.

On a decorative plate or shallow serving dish or platter, place the hummus, garnishing with a dash of Aleppo Pepper or paprika for color, fresh parsley and a thin drizzle of olive oil.

Either of the above garnishes is optional according to individual taste. Serve with wedges of warm pita bread for spreading or dipping.

Cook's Notes: All of the spices and seasonings are subjective. I don't believe any one cook makes her hummus the same. Experiment with the seasonings you like best. For the best flavor, I use fresh spices ground in my spice grinder.

Dried chickpeas may be soaked overnight, drained and then cooked in water along with one tablespoon of baking soda. Cover for an hour or more until tender but still firm. Drain and reserve the liquid. Remove the skins and proceed as above.

My grandmother used the canned version later on and we found no great difference in the taste. Tahini, which is ground sesame paste, is available at all health food and Middle Eastern stores.

Hummus and Mahamara

Mahamara is known throughout the Middle East, with as many different versions. Aleppo is known for the hot peppery version. Although my grandmother's recipe is a mild and slightly sweet version that adults and kids both love, this red pepper spread gets its kick from the tamarind syrup. I have no idea if it is a family alternative or maybe a lesser-known Aleppian version. Whatever the origin many years ago, it is unique.

As a youngster, I loved it because it satisfied my wish for a snack as I ate my vegetables, never knowing how good it was for me. As was her habit of cooking anything, Sitto only made this spread when red peppers were in season, abundant and inexpensive. Today's cook will find sweet red peppers year-round.

SWEET RED PEPPER SPREAD
MAHAMARA

1	CUP OF WALNUT HALVES, TOASTED AND CHOPPED
3	LARGE RIPE SWEET RED PEPPERS
1	BOX ZWIEBACK OR HOLLAND RUSK TOAST (12)
1/8	CUP LEMON JUICE (JUICE OF 1 LEMON) OR RECONSTITUTED LEMON JUICE
1/8	TEASPOON SALT
1/3	CUP VEGETABLE OIL (MORE MAY BE ADDED IF NEEDED)
1/4	CUP TAMARIND SYRUP (SEE BASICS)
1/4	CUP PINE NUTS (OPTIONAL)

See the Cook's Notes for tips on toasting the walnuts.

Rinse the raw peppers. Remove the core and seeds and discard. Slice the peppers in quarters.

In a food processor fitted with a metal blade or a grinder attachment on a KitchenAid mixer: Grind the peppers, alternating with the Zwieback toasts. This will look like a puree. Add the lemon juice, salt, oil and tamarind syrup.

Remove to a bowl and then add the nuts and mix well until the mixture is a spreading consistency. The oil content may be increased or decreased, to taste. Add the pine nuts, if preferred.

Chill the spread in a tightly covered container before serving. The spread should keep about 1 week.

This healthy vegetable spread is delicious on pita bread as a sandwich. It can also be used as a cocktail spread on crusty toasted bread or crackers and makes an interesting dip for fresh vegetables.

Cook's Notes: To toast walnut halves in the oven: Place them on a lipped baking sheet. Bake at 350 degrees until the nuts darken and become fragrant. Stir and stay with them, as they can burn quickly. If broiling, they need constant attention and should be ready in a few minutes. During either process, stir to brown evenly. Walnuts can also be toasted, stove-top, in a dry skillet. Watch and stir frequently.

If you have difficulty finding Zwieback or Holland Rusk Toasts, I have tried Pogen Original Swedish Toasts called Krispolls, a dry toast, thicker than Melba Toast and richer tasting. Trader Joe's Brioche Toast also works well.

To make your own Zwieback: Use any quality bread slices (except multi-grain), cut each slice into thirds. Lay flat on a baking sheet and bake at 250 degrees for 3 to 4 hours until brown and dry.

Sweet Red Pepper Spread

Danny Thomas Fundraiser For St. Jude Hospital.

Every winter, our church would have an evening gala, called a Hafla. This evening gathering of the whole Syrian and Lebanese community was always exciting. Families would all attend, dressing to the nines, relishing the ethnic food and music. There was always an Arabic ensemble or Naubi, usually with a well-known recording artist singing the native songs as the young men and women danced. The church's Ladies' Social Club always prepared all of the marvelous Syrian foods and sweets. Each table would be laden with several Mezze dishes, like Ful Moudammas, along with Hummus, Kibbe Nai, Jibneh and Khubiz.

I remember one particularly special Hafla in Brooklyn, New York, at the St. George Hotel. It was a huge fundraiser led by Danny Thomas. He was launching St. Jude Hospital and this Hafla would be for this new undertaking. Several groups from the metropolitan New York and New Jersey area attended this fun event. We loved Danny, one of our successful Arab sons. The setting was so glamorous, with great music and food, with lots of friends and family to see. As a young woman, I was star-struck!

FAVA BEAN DIP
FUL MOUDAMMAS

1	15 OZ. CAN FAVA BEANS
2	CLOVES OF GARLIC
1/2	TEASPOON SALT, OR TO TASTE
1	TABLESPOON OLIVE OIL, OR MORE TO TASTE
1/2	LEMON
1/2	TEASPOON GROUND CUMIN
	PINCH ALEPPO PEPPER
	FRESH CHOPPED PARSLEY

Fava Bean Dip

Heat the beans and liquid in a 2 qt. saucepan and set aside.

Crush the garlic and the salt in a mortar and pestle or use a garlic press and then add the salt, if this is more convenient.

Mash the beans in some of their liquid and add the garlic paste and the olive oil. Squeeze the 1/2 lemon into the beans and the cumin. Taste the seasonings and adjust, as desired. Spoon the dip onto a serving plate and sprinkle with the Aleppo Pepper and parsley, to garnish.

Cook's Notes: White beans can be substituted for an updated alternate version.

This well-known vegetable dip is made and loved in every country throughout the Middle East. While the basic ingredients are the same, each regional cook will season it differently. Although it's a staple on the Mezze table, my grandmother would often have it as a lunch with Syrian bread.

EGGPLANT DIP
BABA GHANOUJ

1	**LARGE EGGPLANT**
2	**GARLIC CLOVES**
1	**TEASPOON SALT**
1/2	**FRESH LEMON, JUICED**
1/4	**CUP TAHINI**
	DASH GROUND CUMIN
	DASH ALEPPO PEPPER
1	**TABLESPOON FRESH PARSLEY, CHOPPED**
	OLIVE OIL

Eggplant Dip

Pierce the eggplant in a few places. Grill the eggplant under the broiler or on top of a grill, turning frequently, until it is charred and softened. It will collapse. Set aside to cool.

In a mortar and pestle, pound the garlic with the salt until it is a paste. Or, use a garlic press and then add the salt to it.

When the eggplant is cool enough to handle, cut the top off. Slice the eggplant in half and scoop out the pulp into a bowl. Remove the seeds and drain any liquids. Using a potato masher, coarsely puree the eggplant.

Add the garlic paste, lemon juice, tahini and ground cumin. Taste the seasonings and adjust, if desired. Some olive oil may be needed for a thinner or smoother texture.

Place in a serving dish and finish with a drizzle of olive oil. Then garnish with the Aleppo Pepper and chopped parsley.

Serve with quartered pita bread (Khubiz).

Cook's Notes: An additional garlic clove, more tahini or lemon juice may be added to taste. The seasonings are typically at the cook's discretion.

I can remember my grandmother trying to suggest a quick lunch for me when there wasn't anything that interested me in the refrigerator. It would be a real peasant lunch, but one that I love today. She would take pita bread (Khubiz) and split it, dribble some oil on it and then a mixture of Zahtar spices, which she prepared and had on hand.

Zahtar spice is available pre-mixed at Middle Eastern markets. I also see it today made up as a kind of a pizza in Middle Eastern stores. The spices are rubbed onto oiled pita bread and sold as my grandmother made it for me. This would make a great appetizer bread with olives for Mezze, as well. Why not prepare any leftover dough with this spice blend?

SPICE BREAD
ZAIT W' ZAHTAR

1	RECIPE BASIC BREAD DOUGH (KHUBIZ) PAGE 4
	OLIVE OIL
	ZAHTAR SPICES
	SALT, TO TASTE (OPTIONAL)

Spice Bread

Prepare the dough per the basic Syrian bread recipe on page 4 in Basics.

If Zahtar spices are not available or you prefer to blend them yourself, try my homemade Zahtar spice blend in this suggested ratio:

4	TABLESPOONS DRIED THYME
2	TEASPOONS GROUND SUMAC
1/2	TEASPOON SALT, OR MORE TO TASTE
1	TABLESPOON WHITE SESAME SEED, OR MORE TO TASTE
2	TEASPOONS DRIED MINT
1	TEASPOON CORIANDER SEEDS, GROUND FRESH
1/4	TEASPOON FENNEL SEEDS, GROUND FRESH

Combine and blend all the spices, by hand, then add the sesame seeds to make approximately 1/4 to 1/3 cup.

Depending on the quantity needed, combine the olive oil and spices to form a paste.

Before the bread rounds are ready to bake: Take the bread round and lightly oil the top. Turn it over and then smear the olive oil and spice paste to the top, pressing into the rounds of dough with your fingers.

Follow the recipe for baking bread. Remove from the oven and place in a bag or cloth so the breads do not get hard. It will be fine to stack them.

Or, if the bread is already baked, brush the top with the oil and spice paste. Heat on foil in a 375 degree oven for about 5 minutes. Then enjoy this humble snack or sandwich, renowned throughout Aleppo and the Middle East!

Cook's Notes: Zahtar is an already prepared mixture of ground thyme, white sesame seeds, plus a bit of ground sumac. Sumac gives it a bite and a slightly tart taste. This spice blend will be greenish to brown in color. Although Zahtar spice is also red, Aleppians prefer the green variety. It can be obtained at on-line Middle Eastern sites or stores. Purchase or make in small quantities for the freshest taste.

These are my favorite spices, but you may prefer fewer of these. Conversely, other fragrant spices may be added to this blend, making it your own.

Zahtar spice also works as a spice rub before grilling or roasting some meats or poultry.

These delicious spinach appetizers are much loved by the family. I have prepared them ahead and frozen them, unbaked, on the sheets. It was then a lot easier to have them ready in any quantity for an appreciative crowd.

SPINACH PHYLLO TRIANGLES
SBANIKH B' WARAQ

2	**10 OZ. PACKAGES CHOPPED SPINACH (FROZEN)**
1	**MEDIUM YELLOW ONION, DICED**
2	**TABLESPOONS OLIVE OIL**
1/2	**TEASPOON GROUND CUMIN**
3 - 4	**CLOVES GARLIC, CRUSHED**
1/2	**TEASPOON SALT, OR MORE TO TASTE**
1	**8 OZ. PKG. FETA CHEESE, CRUMBLED**
2	**EGGS, BEATEN**
1	**LB. PACKAGE PHYLLO PASTRY**
1/2	**LB. MARGARINE OR BUTTER, MELTED**

Cook the spinach according to the package directions. Cool and drain through a strainer squeezing out all the water and place into a 3 qt. bowl. Set aside.

In a 10" skillet, sauté the onion in olive oil. When lightly browned, add to the cooled spinach. Add the cumin, garlic, salt, and feta cheese and mix well. Taste the seasonings and adjust, if necessary. Then add the eggs. Set aside.

Preheat the oven to 400 degrees. Prepare a lipped baking sheet by greasing it with some butter.

Open the phyllo package. Unroll and cut the rectangular piece in half, lengthwise, cutting through all layers. Put 1/2 of this back in the refrigerator, wrapped in its cellophane or in Saran Wrap.

With the remaining half on your cutting board, cover immediately with a sheet of wax paper and then a slightly dampened kitchen dish towel. The idea is to keep the dough sheets from drying out, which happens in a few minutes. If any sheets are brittle as you go to use them, discard and take from lower in the stack.

Take 2 sheets of phyllo and brush with melted butter. Turn the top sheet over. Then place about 2 tablespoons of filling on the bottom right side of the rectangle. Turn the bottom left side corner over the filling and towards the right, forming a triangle. Repeat this fold up towards the left and then the right again until the phyllo is completely folded into a triangle. If any pieces break off, or the filling is leaking through, just repair with another sheet of phyllo dough.

Phyllo, though fragile, is pretty easy to repair your mistakes, should you make them. Just remember to use melted butter in between every two layers. Place on an ungreased baking sheet about 1" apart and brush the tops with more melted butter. As you need more phyllo dough, remove the dough from the refrigerator, keeping under the damp kitchen towel as you work.

Bake the triangles at 400 degrees for 15 to 20 minutes, until golden brown. Serve immediately.

If preparing for future use, the triangles can be made and buttered on the baking sheets, covered with foil and then frozen.

When ready to bake, do not defrost. Bake longer than the 15 to 20 minutes, just until golden brown.

Cook's Notes: Phyllo can be purchased in one pound boxes in the freezer case of most supermarkets and in Middle Eastern stores.

Frozen phyllo should be defrosted slowly in its package in the refrigerator for up to 8 hours or the day before using.

A fast thaw will cause condensation in the pastry package. Do not refreeze after defrosting. Wrap any leftover defrosted phyllo in airtight plastic bags and store in the refrigerator for about 1 week. Unfrozen phyllo should only be left in original packaging at room temperature for up to 4 hours before baking with it.

When handling, keep the opened phyllo covered with plastic wrap or wax paper and then covered with a damp towel to keep the paper-thin sheets from drying out. Open and take out only those sheets you will be immediately working with, keeping the rest wrapped and refrigerated. Any direct draft will also dry out the sheets.

When working with phyllo paper, do not get the phyllo wet before using it. Use sweet or clarified butter or butter no-stick spray between each few layers to allow browning and to keep it from disintegrating. If phyllo tears while preparing a dish, patch it with more phyllo. It is very forgiving.

Spinach Phyllo Triangles

Years ago, the women of Syria made their own Phyllo dough. Today's store-bought versions are terrific and I can't help but wonder how those earlier cooks, lacking modern kitchens, accomplished what they did!

These fragrant meat and tamarind-filled "finger" rolls will be a great addition to your Mezze table. They can be made ahead and baked when needed as an appetizer or a unique luncheon dish along with a salad.

MEAT-FILLED FINGER ROLLS
ASABIH B' LAHMEH

1	LB. GROUND LAMB OR GROUND BEEF
1	MEDIUM YELLOW ONION, CHOPPED
	TEASPOON SALT
2	TEASPOONS DATAH SPICE (SEE GLOSSARY)
1	CUP CHOPPED TOMATOES, AND JUICE
1	TABLESPOON LEMON JUICE
3 - 4	TABLESPOONS TAMARIND SYRUP
1/4	CUP PINE NUTS
1	LB. PHYLLO DOUGH
1/2	LB. BUTTER OR MARGARINE, MELTED

Meat-Filled Finger Rolls

Mix the meat, onions, salt and Datah spice in a 2 qt. bowl.

In a large 12" skillet or frying pan, sauté this mixture until the meat is cooked and the onions and meat are lightly browned. Add the tomatoes and lemon juice.

Turn off the heat and stir in the tamarind syrup and the pine nuts. Mix and set aside or chill until ready to use.

Preheat oven to 400 degrees. Prepare the phyllo for filling:

Open the phyllo package. After unrolling, cut the large rectangular piece vertically in half, cutting through all layers. Put half of this back in the refrigerator, wrapped in its cellophane or in Saran Wrap.

With the remaining half on your cutting board, cover immediately with wax paper and then a slightly dampened kitchen dish towel. This will keep the dough sheets from drying out, which happens in a few minutes. If any sheets are brittle as you go to use them, discard and take from lower in the stack. Keep any unused sheets covered.

Take 2 sheets of phyllo and brush with melted butter. Turn the top sheet over. Then place about 3 tablespoons of the meat filling evenly down the vertical length of the pastry. Roll into a long finger shape and tuck in each end before completely rolled up. If any pieces break off or the filling is leaking through, just repair with another sheet of phyllo. Remember to use melted butter in between every two layers. As you need more phyllo dough, remove the dough from the refrigerator, keeping the sheets covered as you work.

Place the rolls on a greased or parchment-covered baking sheet about 1" apart and brush the tops with more melted butter. Bake the rolls for 15 to 20 minutes until golden brown. Cut the rolls into smaller serving pieces.

Cook's Notes: If preparing for future use, cover the bottom of a baking sheet with foil and crimp all around. Place the unbaked, rolled and buttered pastries on the sheets, cover with more foil and then freeze. When ready to bake, do not defrost. Bake longer than the 15 to 20 minutes, just until golden brown.

For tips on working with phyllo, see the Cook's Notes in Spinach Finger Rolls.

When the Armenians fled Turkey, many of them settled in Aleppo, Syria. It's interesting to note that their influence has been seen in many of the Aleppo dishes, particularly in the meats and spices. Years ago, my Armenian friend gave me this recipe for traditional Borek, and I've served it ever since for family and guests.

ARMENIAN CHEESE BOREK
JIBNEH B' WARAQ

12	OZ. FETA CHEESE, CRUMBLED
12	OZ. MILD CHEESE, SHREDDED (SEE COOK'S NOTES)
2	EGGS, BEATEN
1/2	TEASPOON SALT, OR TO TASTE
1/4	CUP FRESH PARSLEY, CHOPPED
3	SCALLIONS, CHOPPED
1/2	LB. MARGARINE OR BUTTER, MELTED
1	LB. PHYLLO PASTRY DOUGH

Preheat the oven to 400 degrees.

Prepare a lipped baking sheet by greasing it or use parchment paper.

Mix the cheeses, eggs, salt, parsley and scallions in a 2 qt. bowl. Set aside while you prepare the phyllo sheets.

Open the phyllo package. After unrolling, cut the large rectangular piece vertically, in half, cutting through all layers. Take one rectangle stack to work and put the rest back in the refrigerator, wrapped in cellophane or in Saran Wrap. With the remaining stack on your cutting board, cover immediately with a sheet of wax paper and then a slightly dampened kitchen dish towel.

Take 2 sheets of phyllo and brush with melted butter. Turn the top sheet over. Then place about 1 heaping tablespoon of filling on this rectangle in the lower right corner. Then fold the lower left corner diagonally to the right, forming a triangle. Continue to fold triangles, left and right, all the way up the sheet. There will be a slight overage at the top. Butter this and then tuck under the triangular roll and place it on the baking sheet.

Remember to use melted butter in between every two layers. Place on a baking sheet about 1" apart and brush tops with more melted butter. Bake the Borek at 400 degrees for 8 to 10 minutes. Do not brown the phyllo, as it becomes bitter tasting if browned too much.

Cook's Notes: I've used mild cheeses that melt like Muenster, Jack, mild Cheddar or even a blend of cheeses. I often add a few favorite chopped herbs to the basic cheese mixture.

If preparing for future use, cover the bottom of a baking sheet with foil and crimp all around. Place the unbaked and buttered Borek on the sheets, cover with more foil and then freeze. When baking the frozen Borek, there's no need to defrost, just bake them a bit longer until golden brown.

As a little girl, I always remembered my grandmother's seemingly instant lunches and picnics. One of my favorites was a wonderful cold pickled meat roll that was sliced thin and put into Syrian bread for a quick and satisfying lunch. She would vary the filling, sometimes with a whole boiled egg inside, sometimes with pistachio and pine nuts, which were my favorite. These loaves are wonderful eye-stoppers for appetizers on the Mezze table!

PICKLED LAMB ROLLS
MUTADELLAH

1 1/2	LBS. GROUND LAMB (VERY LEAN, GROUND 3 TIMES)
1	TEASPOON SALT
3	TEASPOONS GROUND ALLSPICE
3	CLOVES CRUSHED GARLIC
1/4	CUP PISTACHIO NUTS, BLANCHED, PEELED AND HALVED (SEE COOK'S NOTES)
1/4	CUP PINE NUTS
3	EGGS, HARD BOILED (OPTIONAL, USE ONLY IN PLACE OF NUTS)

Mix the ground lamb, salt, allspice and garlic in a 3 qt. bowl and shape into three balls. See Cook's Notes.

On wax paper, firmly flatten each ball to 1/2" thickness with your hands. Sprinkle the pistachio and pine nuts equally over each flattened ball.

Then shape the meat into cylinders by rolling the paper to firmly form a 4" long cylinder, enclosing the nuts into the center of each one. Use cold water again on your hands to smooth the outside of the loaves.

If using an egg, eliminate the nuts and put an egg into the center of each of the three meat cylinders. Set aside and prepare the pickling liquid.

For the pickling:

5	CUPS COLD WATER
2 1/2	CUPS WHITE VINEGAR
1	TABLESPOON SALT

Place the water, vinegar and salt in a large 5 qt. pan and bring to a boil. Lower the heat to a simmer and add the meat rolls to cook for about 15 minutes. Turn off the heat, drain and cool. Refrigerate or freeze in baggies for future use.

Each chilled meat loaf can be sliced into thin or medium thick slices for sandwiches or as a unique appetizer accent on the Mezze table.

Cook's Notes: A small 1 qt. bowl of ice water is helpful in shaping the rolls and preventing them from sticking to your hands.

To Blanch Pistachios:
Shell and pour boiling water over them. Steep the nuts for a few minutes before draining and cooling. Peel the skins by rubbing them. Let dry.

Pickled Lamb Rolls

My father-in-law taught me how to make these wonderful pickled turnips, which are a staple on the Syrian table. This is a vegetable I can't even bring myself to eat any other way. They will add a colorful and healthy accompaniment to sandwiches, dinner or Mezze. Even the kids will love eating something pink and good for them!

PICKLED TURNIPS
LIFT MEKHALEL

2 1/2	LBS. FRESH TURNIPS (APPROXIMATELY 8 MEDIUM SIZE)
1	14 OZ. CAN WHOLE BEETS, DRAINED, RESERVING BEET LIQUID
4	CUPS BOILED WATER
1 3/4	TABLESPOONS SALT
3	CUPS WHITE VINEGAR, OR TO TASTE
4	GLASS JARS 32 OZ. WITH LIDS (CLEAN AND STERILE)

Wash off the turnips under hot running water and scrub the outside. Cut the ends and beards off. Make an X cross-cut in the top of each turnip.

Put approximately 3 turnips and one whole beet into wide-mouth jars. Depending on the size of the jar, you may fit more or less. In fact, if you have difficulty fitting a large turnip, cut it in half to fit in the jar. Set aside.

Make a brine solution consisting of the boiled water, which has been cooled, salt and vinegar. Add a little beet liquid to the brine for color. This solution can be increased, using the above ratio, in order to fill the jars enough to cover the turnips.

Cover each jar with lids. Store in a cool area, at room temperature for one to two weeks. Taste for salt and optimal pickling flavor at one week and adjust if necessary. When pickled, the turnips will be crunchy and prettier than nature made them...becoming a lovely shade of magenta pink ...and the pickled beets are a bonus!

Cook's Notes: You may prefer to peel the skin before eating them. However, the skins are perfectly edible after pickling. Cut in wedges to serve.

Option: Cauliflowerets may also be pickled this way in separate jars. Eliminate the beets and beet liquid. Add a teaspoon of pickling spice, 1/2 teaspoon of mustard seed, dash of Aleppo Pepper and a clove of garlic to the brine liquid.

To clean jars best: I recommend running the jars and lids through the dishwasher with a heat cycle. Remove warm jars and fill.

Pickled Turnips

SALADS AND DRESSINGS

Sitto, her sister, Zekeya and their friends always compared recipes. I often remember them discussing who puts how much of this or that into a dish, each cook so sure that her ratio was the right one.

It was on one of those wonderful summer days in Garrett Mountain that I first remembered tasting Aunt Zekeya Farraye's wonderful salad. Although I've tasted many variations of this staple salad of the Middle East, my aunt's remains the best for just the right ingredients. I do remember that her version looked less green than most, probably because her ratio of Bulgar Wheat was more generous. Yours may be a bit different, but that's what each cook gives to a recipe anyway. Here's to Aunt Zekeya's Tabbouleh! Have fun making it your very own!

AUNT ZEKEYA'S TABBOULEH SALAD
TABBOULEH MIN KHALI ZEKEYA

1 1/2	CUPS BULGAR WHEAT (#1 FINE GRAIN ONLY)
1	BUNCH PARSLEY LEAVES, CHOPPED
1	CUCUMBER, MEDIUM, SEEDED AND CUBED
2	TOMATOES, RIPE, CUBED
5	SCALLIONS, CHOPPED FINELY
4	TABLESPOONS OLIVE OIL
1/4	TEASPOON GROUND CUMIN
2	TEASPOONS GROUND ALLSPICE, OR TO TASTE
1/2	TEASPOON SALT, OR TO TASTE
1/4	CUP MINT, FRESH, CHOPPED
1	LEMON, HALVED

Place the Bulgar wheat in a 4 cup glass measuring cup. Fill the cup with cold water and allow the Bulgar to settle to the bottom. Drain off the water and repeat several more times until the water appears clean and clear. Then add about 1 more cup of fresh water and set aside for about 1 hour while you prepare the salad.

Aunt Zekeya's Tabbouleh Salad

Place the cubed cucumber in a colander, lightly salt and set aside for 15 minutes to allow the water to seep out of it.

Drain any remaining water from the wheat and squeeze dry. Add the olive oil, spices, salt and mint. Combine all of the vegetables with the Bulgar wheat and spices.

Squeeze only half of the lemon into the salad and toss. Add more lemon to taste, if desired.

Cook's Notes: All the spices should be to your taste. You may want to add more or less. Serve with pita bread and/or romaine lettuce leaves to be used as spoons.

Bulgar wheat (Burghul) is available in Middle Eastern and health food stores in fine to coarse grains.

Every meal my grandmother prepared was preceded by a dish of freshly cut raw vegetables. We would munch on the colorful offerings while we awaited our lunch or dinner. In fact, Sitto always planned her meals around vegetables, rather than meats. My love of beets surely comes from the fact that she served this salad often.

BEET SALAD
SALATIT SHAWANDAR

5	**FRESH BEETS**
1 1/2	**TEASPOONS SALT (DIVIDED USE)**
	DASH PEPPER
4	**TABLESPOONS OLIVE OIL**
3	**TABLESPOONS WHITE VINEGAR OR LEMON JUICE**
1/2	**TEASPOON GROUND ALLSPICE**
	DASH ALEPPO PEPPER (OPTIONAL)
1	**ONION, THINLY SLICED**
	CHOPPED FRESH PARSLEY OR MINT FLAKES (OPTIONAL)

Beet Salad

Preheat the oven to 400 degrees.

Cut off the tops of the beets, rinse and scrub.

Place the beets in a small baking pan and season all with 1 teaspoon of salt and a dash of pepper. Add just enough cold water to cover the bottom of the pan. Cover the pan with foil and bake for 45 minutes to 1 hour or until tender in the center when pierced with a fork.

While the beets are cooking, mix the oil, vinegar or lemon, 1/2 teaspoon salt, allspice, and Aleppo Pepper in a measuring cup. Adjust the seasonings and vinegar to taste. Set aside.

Remove the beets from the oven and let cool in the pan. Drain the liquid and peel the skins. Slice the beets into 1/4" rounds.

In a 4 qt. salad bowl, combine the beets and the sliced onions with the dressing and chill before serving.

Optional: Garnish with parsley or mint flakes, if desired.

I often picture my Sitto in her little yard, always busy with her plants. She had the prerequisite grapevine, of course. There was an old pear tree and a wonderful hyacinth bush we all sat around on warm days. I remember the fragrant honeysuckle vines and of course, her plot of fresh mint, a staple in Syrian cooking. She would pick the mint, rinse the stems and leaves, and then lay them out in flat pans in the sun to dry. She would then run her fingers down the stem and the fragrant dried mint would flake off into clean jars for flavoring meals, just the way it was done in Syria.

This salad always signaled Easter and springtime at Sitto Naima's house. I loved how refreshing this always tasted with warm homemade bread.

Sitto Naima In Her Yard

SPRING YOGURT SALAD
DETBEEL RABI

1	CUCUMBER
2	CLOVES GARLIC, OR TO TASTE
1	TEASPOON FRESH PEPPERMINT OR 3/4 TEASPOON DRIED MINT FLAKES
1/2	TEASPOON SALT, APPROXIMATE (DIVIDED USE)
1	QT. YOGURT, PLAIN, HOMEMADE OR COMMERCIAL
1/2	HEAD ICEBERG LETTUCE - TORN INTO BITE-SIZED PIECES
1 - 2	STALKS GREEN ONION, SLICED

Peel the cucumber and quarter. Place in a colander and sprinkle lightly with salt while you prepare the remaining ingredients.

In a mortar and pestle: Pound the garlic, peppermint and remaining salt to form a paste. If preferred, use a blender or a garlic press.

In a 3 qt. bowl, add the garlic paste to the yogurt and blend.

Dice the drained cucumber and add to the yogurt along with the lettuce and green onion. Toss and refrigerate to chill for 30 minutes before serving.

Serve as a salad with warm Syrian bread, quartered or serve the yogurt salad with the bread broken into bite-sized pieces sprinkled on top.

Cook's Notes: Rinse and dry the lettuce and green onions before adding into the yogurt.

How we loved our Syrian community's summer church festivals, our Maharajans! Once we unloaded our car, I remember the sounds and smells as we walked down the path to the green meadow below us. Our arms were laden with picnic necessities, as we walked to the tables and barbecue grills scattered about below. I would always hear the music first...a drum...the Dirbekki, the wonderful Oud, a Middle Eastern mandolin, and then I would hear the people laughing. I could already smell the delicious meats cooking on the grills. The smoke would be wafting up towards our path as we anticipated what Sitto would have for us to grill. We met aunts and uncles, cousins, friends and it would be like one giant family reunion, as we all shared laughs, stories and great food. The older generation was always asking about those who were still in Syria, sharing stories of their old hometown, and talking about newly arrived friends and family.

My grandmother made potato salad the Syrian way, with parsley and allspice and then later made an American version that was equally delicious. We have enjoyed both salads. The later version follows.

SYRIAN POTATO SALAD
SALATIT BUTATA SHAMI

5	WHITE POTATOES, RINSED AND SCRUBBED
1/2	CUP OLIVE OIL
1/2	CUP LEMON JUICE
1	CUP CHOPPED PARSLEY
1	TEASPOON SALT, OR TO TASTE
1/2	TEASPOON GROUND ALLSPICE, OR MORE TO TASTE
	DASH ALEPPO PEPPER (OPTIONAL)
	DASH GROUND CORIANDER (OPTIONAL)

Syrian Potato Salad

In a 4 qt. saucepan, cover the potatoes with cold water. Bring to a boil and then simmer until tender and cooked but still firm. Drain and cool enough to handle and then peel and cut into 1/8" thick round slices. Place in a salad bowl.

Mix the oil, lemon juice, parsley, salt and allspice in a measuring cup. Pour over the potatoes and chill for a few hours.

Serve chilled with a sprinkle of the Aleppo Pepper and a dash of ground coriander, if desired.

Cook's Notes: I use fresh spices ground in my spice grinder for the best flavor.

Sitto made this potato salad more often in the later years. I think it was because we all loved it and it continues to get rave reviews from the younger generation. It's now considered my potato salad by my children and grandchildren, but I remember my grandmother, Naima, every time I make it.

SITTO'S POTATO SALAD
SALATIT BUTATA MIN SITTO

8 - 9	**MEDIUM POTATOES, WHITE OR RED – NOT RUSSET OR BAKING**
4	**STALKS CELERY, CHOPPED**
4	**CARROTS, GRATED**
2	**MEDIUM YELLOW ONIONS, GRATED**
1 1/2	**CUPS MAYONAISE**
1/4	**CUP WHITE VINEGAR, UP TO 1/4 CUP, MORE TO TASTE**
	SALT AND PEPPER, TO TASTE

Scrub the potatoes and place in a large 5 qt. pot with cold water. Bring to a boil. Gently simmer until tender but not soft. Drain and cool enough to handle.

Peel and cut the potatoes into large, bite-sized pieces. Some may break while blending, so don't cut them too small. Place them in a large 4 qt. salad bowl. Mix in all the remaining ingredients and taste to make any adjustments.

Cook's Notes: I usually add more than the 1/4 cup of vinegar. Be cautious with the salt until all is mixed and taste again before adjusting, as the vinegar can replace much of the salt.

Chill the salad for a few hours before serving.

Great grandmother Lucy was a pretty emancipated woman. As the story goes, when she had a disagreement with great grandfather, she'd straighten her back and tell him, "Remember, I am an Abdelnour." It's clear she wanted to remind him that she was no peasant!

This humble peasant salad is something you can make your own. While the herbs and seasonings are typical, the vegetables can be any you prefer. Sitto preferred iceberg lettuce, but romaine is traditional.

BREAD SALAD
FATTOUSH

1	HEAD LETTUCE, TORN
2	VINE-RIPENED TOMATOES, DICED
1	CUCUMBER, DICED
1	BUNCH RADISHES, SLICED
1/2	RED ONION, DICED

Dressing:

2	CLOVES GARLIC
1/2	TEASPOON SALT, OR TO TASTE
1/3	CUP OLIVE OIL
1/4	CUP FRESH LEMON JUICE
3	STEMS FRESH MINT LEAVES, CHOPPED
4	STEMS FRESH PARSLEY, LEAVES CHOPPED
	DASH ZAHTAR SPICE (SEE GLOSSARY)
1/4	CUP KALAMATA OR RIPE OLIVES
1	PITA BREAD, TOASTED

Combine the vegetables in a large 4 qt. salad bowl and chill while you prepare the dressing.

Pound the garlic and salt in a mortar and pestle or a garlic press to make a paste. Set aside.

Bread Salad

In a 2 cup bowl or measuring cup, combine the olive oil, lemon juice, mint and parsley. Then add the garlic paste, a dash of Zahtar spice and mix well. Taste and adjust the seasonings. Then add the olives to the dressing and set aside.

Break the toasted bread into bite-sized pieces and when ready to serve, pour the dressing over the greens, mixing in the bread pieces.

This lemon dressing was my grandmother's daily salad dressing. It was always light, refreshing and typical of the Aleppo spices she favored.

SYRIAN LEMON DRESSING
ZAIT LAIMUN SHAMI

1	**CLOVE GARLIC**
1/2	**TEASPOON SALT**
2	**LEMONS, JUICED, SEEDS REMOVED**
1/4	**CUP OLIVE OIL**
1	**TABLESPOON CHOPPED FRESH PARSLEY**
1/2	**TEASPOON GROUND ALLSPICE**
1/4	**TEASPOON GROUND CORIANDER**
	ALEPPO PEPPER OR BLACK PEPPER, TO TASTE

Crush the garlic and salt in a mortar and pestle to form a paste or use a garlic press, if preferred. Combine the garlic paste and the remaining ingredients in a measuring cup or small bowl and chill before serving.

Cook's Notes: For the freshest taste, use whole spices ground in a spice grinder. Use fresh coriander leaves, if preferred.

This traditional dressing is a staple in the Middle East. It's used over Kibbe as a sauce and can be a great appetizer dip for the Mezze table.

SESAME TAHINI DRESSING
TAHINEH

2	**CLOVES GARLIC**
1/2	**TEASPOON SALT, OR TO TASTE**
1/4	**CUP WATER OR MORE, IF NEEDED**
1/2	**CUP TAHINI**
1/2	**LEMON, JUICED**
2	**TABLESPOONS CHOPPED FRESH PARSLEY**
	DASH GROUND CUMIN (OPTIONAL)

Crush the garlic and salt together in a mortar and pestle. Or, use a blender or garlic press and add the salt to the crushed garlic.

In a small 1 qt. bowl, combine the water with the tahini to blend well. Add the garlic and salt, lemon juice and parsley. Adjust with more water, if needed. The mixture will thicken more when chilled. Taste for seasoning and adjust. Add the dash of cumin, if desired. Chill the dressing for an hour.

Serve over salad greens or grilled vegetables. The dressing may be thinned with a little more water, if needed.

Cook's Notes: For an appetizer dip, eliminate the water. Serve with pita bread triangles or fresh vegetables.

I remember helping Sitto pick fresh mint in her yard. She kept up with this prolific plant by trimming the stems often. She'd rinse the stems and leaves and dry them in the spring and summer sun. When they were dried, she'd run her fingers down each stem as the dried leaves fell into a jar for year-round use.

YOGURT DRESSING
SULSAH LABAN

1/2	QT. YOGURT (HOMEMADE OR PLAIN COMMERCIAL BRAND)
1	STALK GREEN ONION, SLICED THIN
2	CLOVES GARLIC, CRUSHED, MORE OR LESS TO TASTE
1	TEASPOON FRESH PEPPERMINT OR 1/2 TSP. DRIED MINT FLAKES
1/2	TEASPOON SALT, OR MORE TO TASTE

In a mortar and pestle, pound the garlic, salt and mint into a paste. If preferred, use a blender.

Combine the paste and the green onions into the yogurt. Chill for a few hours and serve over any mixed greens. Water or olive oil may be added to thin it, if preferred.

Cook's Notes: This is a terrific low-calorie dressing which can also be used as a filling for celery, or as a dip for crudités such as raw carrots, broccoli, cucumber, cauliflower, kohlrabi and radishes. Serve with pita chips.

This is also delicious with any of the baked or grilled Kibbe dishes.

I will always remember that wonderful aroma as I walked into Sitto's kitchen. It was most definitely due to her daily use of spices. She, like all Aleppo cooks, could never do without those fragrant and aromatic spices of her homeland.

On one particular day, as I watched her mixing some ground lamb in a bowl, she picked up her glass jar of mixed spices, which she called Datah. She saw that I was intent on learning and she brought the open jar up to my nose so that I could catch the scent. That was it...I was hooked on spices! From that day forward, I have had a real respect for their marvelous influences on a dish. Those spices delivered a deeper flavor to everything and always "told" you the region where they came from and its customary cooking. These Syrian cooks knew this and were never without their spices.

SYRIAN SPICE BLEND
DATAH

2	TEASPOONS GROUND ALLSPICE
1	TEASPOON CINNAMON
1	TEASPOON CUMIN SEED
1/2	TEASPOON GRATED NUTMEG
1/2	TEASPOON GROUND CLOVES
1/2	TEASPOON CARDAMOM SEEDS
1/4	TEASPOON CORIANDER SEEDS
1/8	TEASPOON ALEPPO PEPPER
1/8	TEASPOON BLACK PEPPER

Combine all to a fine grind in a blender or a spice grinder. Store in a tightly covered glass jar. Makes 1/8 cup. Use when called for in a recipe, as a spice mix or rub.

Cook's Notes: For best results, grind these spices in this smaller ratio to keep them at their freshest.

The cardamom seeds should be removed from their pods before grinding or use already-ground cardamom.

Allspice is very difficult to grind, so use already-ground allspice.

Be sure to grate the nutmeg before adding it to the blender. Or, if preferred, use already-ground nutmeg.

Any of these spices can be increased or decreased according to your taste. Every Syrian cook has their own favored version of this blend.

The purchased blend is also known as Baharat and will vary with each vendor.

SOUPS

Years ago, Catholics had to abstain from eating meats on Fridays. Sitto would always serve a healthy vegetarian meal like this soup on those nights. This thick, delicious and satisfying meal would be ready in about an hour.

LENTIL NOODLE SOUP
RISHTAYA ADDES

1 1/4	CUPS BROWN LENTILS
8	CUPS WATER
2	CUPS MEDIUM EGG NOODLES
1	TABLESPOON SALT, OR TO TASTE
	PEPPER, TO TASTE
2	MEDIUM YELLOW ONIONS
1/4	CUP OLIVE OIL
1	CLOVE GARLIC, CRUSHED
1	TEASPOON DRIED PEPPERMINT FLAKES

Lentil Noodle Soup

Sort the lentils, removing any stones. Wash the lentils three times and drain. Place them in a 5 qt. soup pot with the cold water. Cover and bring to a boil. Lower the heat to a simmer until cooked, approximately 20 to 25 minutes. Depending on the age of the lentils, you may need to initially cook them more or less.

When the lentils are cooked, add the noodles to the soup and simmer. Add the salt and pepper and taste to adjust the seasoning. Continue simmering until the noodles are cooked.

Slice the onions vertically into thin slices.

Heat the oil and fry the onions until they are brown and caramelized.

Before the onions are finished, add the crushed garlic clove to the browned onions, stirring well to blend the garlic. Lightly cook for a few minutes. Remove from the heat. Carefully spoon the sautéed onion/garlic mixture into the soup and stir.

Add the mint flakes and simmer a few minutes more. Serve with salad, Syrian bread and enjoy.

Cook's Notes: Lentils do not need to be soaked before cooking. Sitto used the large brown lentils. I have not been able to find them locally, but they are available at Middle Eastern on-line markets.

Some of the lentils will break up and give body to the soup, which is desirable. If you prefer thinner soup, add an additional cup of water after the lentils are cooked and prior to adding the noodles and the rest of the ingredients.

My mother-in-law, Mary, made this chicken soup to the great delight of the family. It was often the starter for Sunday dinner, followed by her Chicken with Rice and Tomatoes, which I included in the Meat and Poultry chapter. I think this delicious soup stands on its own with a salad for lunch or a light dinner.

MARY'S CHICKEN TOMATO SOUP
SHORBAT DJAAJ MA' BANADURA MIN MARY

10	OZ. VERMICELLI NOODLES, OR CUT FIDEO NOODLES, CRUMBLED
8	CUPS CHICKEN STOCK, HOMEMADE OR PURCHASED
1	TEASPOON SUGAR
1/2	TEASPOON BLACK PEPPER
1/4	TEASPOON ALEPPO PEPPER OR RED PEPPER FLAKES
1	TEASPOON SALT
3	CLOVES OF GARLIC, SLIVERED
1	6 OZ. CAN TOMATO PASTE (USE HALF)
1	28 OZ. CAN WHOLE PLUM TOMATOES

Place the crumbled noodles in a baking pan and toast to a dark brown, turning frequently, to prevent burning them. This dark color flavors the soup nicely. Set aside.

Pour the stock into a 5 qt. pot. Add the sugar, black pepper, Aleppo Pepper, salt, garlic, the half can of tomato paste and the whole can of plum tomatoes, which have been squeezed or lightly crushed to break them up.

Boil the soup for 5 minutes. Then add the browned noodles, stir and lower the burner to a simmer and cook for 1 hour, with the lid ajar. Check for seasonings during the latter part of the simmer and adjust according to your taste.

Cook's Notes: If homemade stock is preferred, see "Mary's Chicken with Rice and Tomatoes" recipe for her homemade chicken stock. Then proceed with this soup recipe.

Cooked shredded chicken may be added for a heartier soup.

Mary's Chicken Tomato Soup

Lentils were an important staple of the Syrian cook's menu and so many dishes included these healthy legumes. My grandmother always used the large brown lentils. If these are unavailable, use the smaller brown or green lentils, rather than the yellow ones. In either case, this full-bodied delicious soup is a vegetarian delight.

TOMATO LENTIL SOUP
SHORBAT BANADURA MA' ADDES

1	CUP BROWN LENTILS
4	CUPS VEGETABLE BROTH (32 OZ.) WATER OR CHICKEN BROTH
1	CAN WHOLE TOMATOES IN JUICE
1	MEDIUM YELLOW ONION, DICED
3	SCALLIONS, SLICED THIN
1/4	CUP CHOPPED FRESH PARSLEY
3	CLOVES GARLIC, CRUSHED
1	TEASPOON CUMIN SEED, GROUND
1	TEASPOON WHOLE CORIANDER, GROUND
2	CARROTS, SLICED INTO THIN ROUNDS
2	STALKS CELERY WITH LEAVES, SLICED
1 1/2	TEASPOONS SALT
1/2	TEASPOON PEPPER
1/4	TEASPOON ALEPPO PEPPER
1	BAY LEAF
1	CUP CHOPPED BABY SPINACH, FROZEN, OR 2 CUPS FRESH, WASHED SPINACH

Sort the lentils to remove any stones. Rinse and drain.

Place the broth or water into a 5 qt. pot and bring to a boil. Add the lentils and lower the heat to a simmer. Cover and cook for 20 minutes or until they are tender.

Crush the tomatoes, along with the juice, in a blender or processor.

Except for the spinach, add the tomatoes with the rest of the ingredients to the lentils. Cover and simmer for 1 hour.

Taste the seasonings and adjust, if preferred.

Tomato Lentil Soup

Add the spinach, cover and continue simmering for an additional 10 to 20 minutes or until the vegetables and lentils are cooked.

Remove the bay leaf before serving.

Cook's Notes: The acid in the tomatoes will prolong the cooking time of the lentils, so the cooking time may vary.

I use whole spices ground in my spice grinder for the freshest taste.

I remember coming home from school to the delicious aroma of baking bread. Sitto would be at her oven pulling out the scrumptious rounds of homemade Syrian bread. As they baked, she would sprinkle the tops with water to keep them from browning too much. More small mounds of dough waited their turn as they rose under the white cloth sheeting she used for baking. After they baked, she would cover them again in more cloth, so that they wouldn't harden as they cooled. I saw her move with such expertise. It was second nature to her, having baked these breads since she was a girl in Syria.

MEATBALL RICE SOUP
SHORBAT KIBBE W' RIZ

1	RECIPE LAMB TARTAR (KIBBE NAI) PAGE 89
3	CLOVES GARLIC
1 1/2	TEASPOONS SALT
1	MEDIUM YELLOW ONION, CHOPPED
1/4	CUP OLIVE OIL
1	28 OZ. CAN WHOLE TOMATOES
4	CUPS WATER OR BROTH, LAMB OR VEGETABLE
4	CARROTS, PEELED AND SLICED
1/4	CUP FRESH PARSLEY, CHOPPED
1	TEASPOON GROUND CUMIN
1	TEASPOON GROUND CORIANDER
1/2	TEASPOON BLACK PEPPER
1/4	TEASPOON ALEPPO PEPPER, OR TO TASTE
3/4	CUP COOKED RICE

Meatball Rice Soup

Prepare the basic Kibbe Nai recipe and make small 1" meatballs with the mixture. Chill until needed.

In a mortar and pestle, mash the garlic and salt to make a paste. Or, use a garlic press and then add the salt to the crushed garlic. Set aside.

In a 5 or 6 qt. pot, sauté the chopped onion in the olive oil. When they are translucent, add the garlic paste and stir for a few seconds until golden but not browned.

Crush the tomatoes with your fingers, or a blender. Then add them along with the water or broth, carrots, parsley, spices, salt and peppers to the sautéed onions and garlic. Cover and simmer for 45 minutes.

Taste the seasonings and adjust, if necessary. Add the meatballs and simmer for another 25 minutes. Add the cooked rice and continue to simmer for 5 more minutes.

EGGS

Kadirli
Karatepe
Anazarbus
Birthplace of St. Paul
summoned Cleopatra here
B.C., their first meeting
Ceyhan
Misis
Yumurtalık
(Aegae)
İskenderun
Körfezi
İskenderun
(Alexandretta)
Myriandrus
Musa Dağı
Antakya
(Antioch)
Samandağ
(Seleucia)
Ras el Basit
Jisr esh Shughur
Ugarit
Ibn Hani
adhiqiya
La, Laodicea)
Jeble
LATAKIA
Baniyas
El Qadmus
Margat
(Marghab)
Masyaf
(Massiaf)
Arwad
(Aradus)
Tartus (Tortosa)
Amrit (Marathus)
Safita
Krak des Chevaliers
Hamidiya
Halba

The Assyrians disappeared from history,
killed or absorbed by their conquerors
(Jeremiah 46:2)
Sakçagöz
Zencirli (Senjirli)
İslahiye
Osmaniye
Bahçe
Ceyhan
Erzin
Dörtyol
Payas
Syrian Gates
Kırıkhan
Afrin
Amik
Gölü
Reyhanlı
Tell Tayinat
(Atchana) Alalakh
Tell Judeideh
Harim
Yayladağ
Idlib
An important and wealthy city during
the Crusades, Latakia is regaining its
place with a newly-constructed harbor,
a symbol of Syria's modern progress
Sahyun
Haffe
Apamea
Assassin stronghold
during the Crusades
Ma'arret en
Nu'man
Es Sa'an
Hama
(Hamath, Epiphania)
Selemiya
Er Rastan (Arethusa)
Qatna
Homs (Emesa)
Kadesh
Furqlus

Zeugma
Apamea
Halfeti
Nizip
Gaziantep
Nizip
Oguzeli
Birec
Karkamış
(Carchemish)
Jera
Kilis
A'zaz
St. Simeon Stylites lived atop
a 60-foot pillar for 30 years
Memb
Qal'at
Sam'an
El Bab
Muslimiya
Hittite conques
1600 B.C. over
ancient carav
Today's populat
Haleb
(Aleppo, Beroea)
Sfira
Jebbul
Meskene
Es Sabkha
Dibs
(Thapsacus
Shalmaneser III of Assyria claimed
In his battle with 12 Syrian king
Karkar on the Orontes in 853 B.C.
Israelite led 2,000 chariots and 10
infantry in the coalition against
Isriya
Capital of the m
kingdom, a powerf
of the 12th
Gained notoriety in 218
a priest of the sun-god t
Roman emperor for a sho
S
Y
El'Ain
el Beida

Parsley Omelets

My grandmother made this simple peasant omelet with a very surprising main ingredient…parsley…and it was so delicious. I remember her heating up the old pan to cook the omelets, sizzling and plump. The little omelets were made in the Ejjeh pan she had brought with her from Aleppo as a young girl. That copper-bottomed pan, which is in my kitchen today, has eight round indentations in it for frying the individual 3" omelets. I later likened the pan to the Danish Ebelskiver pan. The little omelets are the perfect size to fit a few into a pita pocket, which is the way she used to serve them, piping hot or later served cold for the next day's lunch or a picnic.

PARSLEY OMELETS
EJJEH MA' BAQDUNIS

6	LARGE EGGS
2	CLOVES GARLIC, CRUSHED
1	MEDIUM YELLOW OR WHITE ONION, CHOPPED
2	TEASPOONS GROUND ALLSPICE
1	TEASPOON SALT
2	TEASPOONS PEPPERMINT FLAKES, DRIED
1	BUNCH FRESH PARSLEY, CHOP THE LEAVES ONLY
	VEGETABLE OR OLIVE OIL FOR FRYING

Beat the eggs and then combine the garlic, onion, allspice, salt, peppermint flakes and chopped parsley.

Heat the Ejjeh pan with 1 teaspoon of oil in each indentation. (See Cook's Notes.)

Drop 2 tablespoons of the egg mixture into the hot oil and sauté for about 2 minutes, until the underside of the omelet appears to be browned; then turn and cook the other side for an additional 1 or 2 minutes. Serve hot or cold in pita bread.

Cook's Notes: An Ejjeh pan is available at some Middle Eastern stores. The next best option is the Ebelskiver pan, which is available online through cooking sites.

If using the Ebelskiver pan, you may find it easier to turn the little omelets during cooking with wooden chopsticks or fondue forks.

A 6" sauté pan may be used as the third alternative. In this case, use about 3 or 4 tablespoons of the egg mixture. The omelet should be about 3" to 4" in diameter.

I've tried the food processor to make quicker work of the chopped parsley and onion but decided that hand chopping is best. The texture of the omelets was too refined and not at all like the original version.

One day, after enjoying another kind of omelet that Sitto made, I asked her what was in it. She pointed to her temple and said "Zwaz." My eyes grew wide and I repeated in English "brains?" When she replied yes in Arabic, I vowed to never eat those poor lamb's brains again! These little omelets, however, were another favorite of mine and especially my sister's.

I remember Sitto cutting out the prickly insides of an artichoke...it seemed so mysterious to me because all of it looked so inedible! But soon she would be preparing it for any number of meat or vegetable dishes. My favorite way was in this omelet because she used only the best part for this dish, the heart.

HEARTS OF ARTICHOKE OMELET
EJJEH MA' SHOKE

1	LEMON, HALVED
4	CUPS COLD WATER, LARGE
2	ARTICHOKES, FRESH
1	TEASPOON SALT

Prepare acidulated water for the artichoke soak:

Fill a 3 qt. bowl half-way with the cold water and the juice of 1/2 of the lemon. Drop in the lemon half, as well. Set aside. This soak will prevent discoloration.

Prepare the artichokes by slicing off the stem to about 1" with a sharp paring knife. Peel the stem end. Tear off and discard the large outer leaves. While placing the artichoke on its side, cut off the tops of the leaves, leaving the lower half of the leaves intact.

Then cut the artichoke in half lengthwise. Clean out the pinkish prickly center with a sharp, pointed knife and also clean out the fuzzy choke, carefully, to remove it all and discard. Take care not to cut into the meaty heart. Immediately drop the artichoke into the lemon water and soak while preparing the second artichoke.

Then rinse both artichokes to clean well. Place in a 2 qt. saucepan, in water to cover, along with the juice of the remaining lemon half and the salt. Bring to a boil, and then simmer, covered, until the hearts are just firm but cooked. Drain and set aside to cool.

When cooled, remove all the leaves. Refrigerate and use later with drawn butter or your favorite dip. Reserve the hearts and remaining base of the stem for the omelet, slice and set aside.

To prepare the omelet:

4	LARGE EGGS
1/4	TEASPOON SALT, OR TO TASTE
1	GARLIC CLOVE, CRUSHED
1/2	TEASPOON GROUND ALLSPICE, OR TO TASTE
	SLICED ARTICHOKE HEARTS
	OLIVE OIL FOR FRYING

In a 2 qt. bowl, beat the eggs, salt, garlic and allspice. Take the sliced artichoke hearts and place into the egg mixture and stir to blend.

In a small 6" sauté pan, heat about 1 tablespoon of the oil and add the egg and artichoke mixture, not quite covering the pan bottom. Sauté until the eggs are beginning to set, turn and finish cooking.

Serve as an omelet or as a sandwich filling in pita bread. This is also excellent served cold for a picnic lunch.

Talented Syrian family cooks found so many ways to cook with squash. These colorful and plentiful vegetables were always an integral part of our menus as an appetizer or hearty lunch. I can even remember eating these omelets cold on some of our picnics, along with Syrian bread and fresh vegetables.

ZUCCHINI OMELETS
EJJEH MA' KUSA

2 - 3	**CLOVES GARLIC**
1	**TEASPOON SALT**
4	**LARGE EGGS**
1	**TABLESPOON FRESH MINT LEAVES, CHOPPED**
1	**TABLESPOON FRESH PARSLEY LEAVES, CHOPPED**
1/2	**TEASPOON DATAH SPICE (SEE GLOSSARY)**
1	**TEASPOON GROUND ALLSPICE**
	DASH ALEPPO PEPPER, OR TO TASTE
1	**ZUCCHINI, GRATED (APPROX. 1 CUP)**
1/2	**CUP ONION, CHOPPED**
	OLIVE OIL FOR FRYING

In a mortar and pestle, mash the garlic and salt to form a paste. Or, use a garlic press and then add the salt to make a paste.

Crack the eggs into a 2 qt. bowl and stir to break the yolks and blend. Add the garlic paste, mint, parsley, Datah spice, allspice and pepper.

Add the grated zucchini and chopped onions to the egg mixture and stir to blend well.

Heat an Ejjeh or Ebelskiver pan with 1 teaspoon of oil in each indentation. (See Cook's Notes.)

Drop 2 tablespoons of the egg mixture into the hot oil and sauté for about 2 minutes, until the underside of the omelet appears to be browned. Then turn and cook the other side for an additional 2 minutes.

Serve warm as a side dish or cold with a salad.

Cook's Notes: An Ejjeh pan is available at some Middle Eastern stores. The next best option is the Ebelskiver pan available at on-line cooking stores.

If using the Ejjeh or Ebelskiver pan, it is helpful to turn the little omelets during cooking with wooden chopsticks, fondue fork or toothpicks.

A 6" sauté pan would be a third alternative. In this case, use about 3 or 4 tablespoons of the egg mixture. The omelet should be about 3" to 4" in diameter.

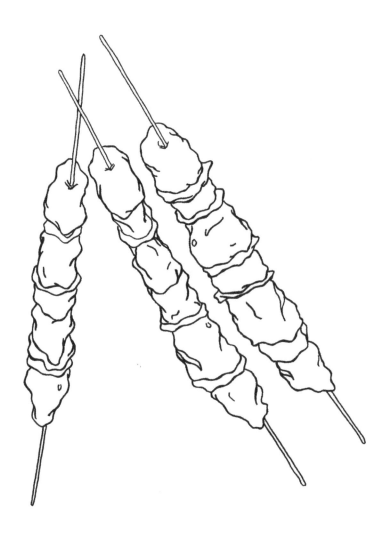

MEAT AND POULTRY

Even at my age, it's hard to believe how steeped in traditional cooking we were in my childhood. In fact, Mom tells the story of one of her early dates with Daddy. She was about 17 years old at the time. They were at a restaurant and he suggested she try the beef. She had to confess that she had never eaten beef. Owing to our ethnic roots, my grandmother prepared lamb exclusively for the family. Mom had never been exposed to this meat until then. Years later, in telling me this story, she did say that she loved the beef. The following dish is not beef, but it is so delicious that it's not so surprising to understand my mother's naivete!

POTTED LEG OF LAMB WITH RICE
SHEDHEH W'RIZ

1	LEG OF LAMB – SHANK PORTION – APPROX. 4 LBS.
2	TABLESPOONS GROUND ALLSPICE
1	HEAD OF GARLIC - PEELED INTO CLOVES
2	TABLESPOONS OLIVE OIL
1	28 OZ. CAN WHOLE TOMATOES, PUREED OR CHOPPED
1	6 OZ. CAN TOMATO PASTE
2	CUPS WATER
1	TEASPOON SALT, OR TO TASTE
	PEPPER, GROUND, TO TASTE
	RICE, PREPARED SEPARATELY, PER PACKAGE

Potted Leg of Lamb with Rice

Slash the lamb leg with 1/2" cuts overall and at random, about 1/2" deep and a few inches apart.

Put the allspice in a small dish and dip your fingers into the allspice and pinch a small amount into each slit along with a garlic clove. (A modern trick is to moisten the garlic, dip into the allspice and then place into each slit.) Any excess allspice may be rubbed over the entire piece of meat. There should be enough slits to accommodate all the garlic cloves.

In a heavy 6 qt. pot or Dutch oven, heat the olive oil and brown the lamb leg on each side.

Add the tomatoes, tomato paste, water, salt and mix well to dissolve the tomato paste. Heat until the mixture begins to boil and then lower to a simmer. Cover and simmer for 2 1/2 to 3 hours until the sauce is thickened and the meat is fork tender.

In the last 20 minutes of cooking, taste for seasoning, adding any additional salt and/or pepper to taste. Cook the rice per package directions.

To serve: Skim any fat on the surface of the sauce before serving. Remove the lamb to a serving platter and slice. Slices can be random and there is no wrong way to carve this. The meat will be very tender and almost falling off the bone. Some slices will contain the garlic which can be eaten or discarded, as desired. Serve accompanied by rice along with a few spoonfuls of the sauce on top of the lamb and rice.

Tamarind or Tamar Hindi in Arabic, gives this dish its unique tart/sweet flavor and the typical Aleppo spices make this fragrant dish so appealing. Sitto always served rice with these Aleppo meatballs, which we considered "comfort food.

TAMARIND MEATBALLS
KABOB TAMAR HINDI

1 1/2	LBS. GROUND LAMB (GROUND ONCE) OR BEEF
1 1/2	TEASPOONS GROUND ALLSPICE
1 1/2	TEASPOONS DATAH SPICE (SEE GLOSSARY)
2	TEASPOONS SALT (DIVIDED USE)
2	TABLESPOONS OLIVE OIL
1	6 OZ. CAN TOMATO PASTE
2 1/2	CUPS WATER
2	TEASPOONS LEMON JUICE
3 - 4	TABLESPOONS TAMARIND SYRUP (SEE BASICS)
2	CARROTS, PEELED AND SLICED

Tamarind Meatballs

In a 2 qt. bowl, mix the ground lamb, allspice, Datah spice and 1 teaspoon of the salt. Moistening your hands, shape into small 1" diameter meatballs.

In a non-stick 12" skillet, heat the oil and brown the meatballs. Remove from the skillet, drain on paper toweling and set aside.

In a 3 qt. saucepan, mix the tomato paste, water, lemon juice, tamarind syrup and 1 teaspoon of the salt and bring to boil. Lower to a simmer and add the meatballs and the sliced raw carrots. Simmer for 45 minutes to an hour until the sauce is thickened and the carrots are tender.

Skim any fat on the surface of the sauce before serving. Serve over cooked rice. This recipe makes about 35 miniature meatballs.

Cook's Notes: Use the lesser amount of tamarind syrup to start and taste at the mid-point. The additional tablespoon can be added, if desired.

Barbequed Lamb Cubes

Whether part of our weekly excursions to Garrett Mountain or a humble back-porch kind of grilling, summer barbeques were never complete without Mishwi. Translated, it is "grilled meat on a skewer." Sitto would rub cubes of lean lamb with ground allspice and then thread the meat onto skewers with onions and grill them. We would wrap the fragrant and delicious grilled lamb with warm homemade Syrian bread as we removed them from the skewers...mmm.

BARBEQUED LAMB CUBES
LAHMEH MISHWI

2	MEDIUM YELLOW ONIONS, QUARTERED
1 1/2	LBS. CUBED LEAN LAMB (FROM LEG)
2	TABLESPOONS OLIVE OIL
1	TEASPOON SALT, OR TO TASTE
1	TABLESPOON GROUND ALLSPICE
1	TEASPOON DATAH SPICE (SEE GLOSSARY)

Cut the lean meat into approximately 1 1/2" cubes and place in a 3 qt. bowl. With your hands, distribute the oil, salt and spices over the meat. Add only about 8 slices of onions to the meat, mixing through to flavor the meat. Reserve the rest of the quartered onions for the skewers when ready to grill. Refrigerate the meat for at least one hour before grilling.

Thread the meat onto the skewers, alternating with the quartered onions, using 2 or 3 layers of the onion at a time. Grill until just cooked through. Do not overcook. Some lamb lovers may prefer pink centers.

Cook's Notes: Sitto used flat rather than round skewers. They are more practical to prevent the meat or veggies from twirling while they grill.

My immigrant grandparents were the anchors of our family. Their love of family, the Arabic language and the foods remembered from their home country kept us all happy and close. In fact, we were so close that I smile thinking back. On hot summer weekends we left, every chance we could, to go to our local Garrett Mountain. We'd pack all kinds of delicious picnic foods and meet family and friends there. It was such a treat because the mountain was so green and cool compared with the crowded houses and streets in downtown Paterson, New Jersey. Later, as I learned about the mountainous beauty of Aleppo, its sour cherry orchards and olive groves and its majestic Citadel high above the city, I could see what my grandparents loved about this lush green mountain above this busy city here in America.

Sitto sometimes prepared a rare delicacy – lamb's liver. After she had marinated it in spices, it was wonderful to enjoy the charcoal-grilled liver cubes served with warmed Syrian bread and salad.

GRILLED LIVER
MATLAT MISHWI

4	**CLOVES GARLIC**
1	**TEASPOON CORIANDER SEED**
1	**TEASPOON DRIED PEPPERMINT FLAKES**
1	**TEASPOON SALT, OR TO TASTE**
1 1/2	**LBS. LAMB'S LIVER CUT INTO 1 1/2" CUBES**
2	**TABLESPOONS OLIVE OIL**
1	**ONION, GRATED FINE**

In a mortar and pestle, blender or food processor:
Crush the garlic, coriander seed, peppermint flakes and salt into a paste.

Rinse the liver, drain and pat dry. Place into a 3 qt. bowl.

Cover the liver cubes with the oil, grated onion and the spice mixture. Marinate for several hours.

Thread onto skewers and grill to medium. Serve with Syrian bread and salad for a summer barbeque.

Cook's Notes: Although other vegetables are not traditional with this dish, you may want to add them for color and/or to balance the dish. Onions, bell peppers or mushrooms are delicious options to grill along with the liver. Cut the peppers and onions into 1" squares so they cook evenly or grill the veggies on their own skewers and grill longer than the liver.

When I was just a girl, I remember my grandmother's porch as just a narrow strip of decking on the third floor of the house my grandparents rented. Those summer days on that porch often included our grilled Aleppo lamb burgers. Fresh Jersey tomatoes and baby cucumbers were just the thing to accompany these burgers on a hot day.

ALEPPO BURGERS
LAHEM MISHWI HALABY

1	LB. GROUND LAMB (LEAN LEG CUT, GROUND ONCE) OR BEEF
1	MEDIUM YELLOW ONION, GRATED
1/4	CUP FRESH CHOPPED PARSLEY
1/2	TEASPOON SALT, OR TO TASTE
1 1/2	TEASPOONS GROUND ALLSPICE

In a 2 qt. bowl, mix the ground lamb and onion, adding the parsley, salt and allspice to blend. Form into patties and grill.

Aleppo Burgers

Homemade Lamb Sausages

Sitto Naima always made her own lamb Sausages which she called Sahseejaw. She'd soak the casings overnight in lemon or orange peels and water. She'd then prepare the meat by grinding lean lamb by hand in her manual grinder attached to the top of the kitchen table. After washing the casings very carefully, turning them inside out, she got out what looked like a big, flat top shaped funnel. She would then begin making the sausages, by hand. No fancy Kitchenaid contraptions in those days! I watched as she'd thread the casings onto the tube of the funnel and with her hands, would fill the cavity with meat, being careful to tie off each sausage as it grew to the right length. When she wasn't grilling them, Sitto used Crisco to fry them, but we can certainly use olive oil today.

I have made these delicious sausages and although they are challenging to make, they are well worth the effort. I think the other possibility would be to make them without casings and just roll the lean meat into cigar shaped rolls and chill before frying in some olive oil. The ground meat mixture can also be molded as a sausage shape around a skewer and grilled. They are addictive!

HOMEMADE LAMB SAUSAGES
SAHSEEJAW

1	CONTAINER LAMB OR SHEEP CASINGS
	ORANGE OR LEMON PEELS
3	LBS. LEAN LAMB, GROUND TWICE
4	TEASPOONS SALT, OR MORE TO TASTE
4 - 5	TABLESPOONS GROUND ALLSPICE
1	TEASPOON DATAH SPICE, OR TO TASTE (SEE GLOSSARY)
2 - 3	CUPS COLD WATER (APPROXIMATELY)

Casings are usually packed in salt. Rinse thoroughly to remove all trace of salt and leave in cold water and orange or lemon peels for several hours or until ready to use the same or next day. To clean the inside of the casings, place one end over a faucet nozzle and gently run cold water through them, being careful not to pierce them with too much water pressure. If any are pierced, cut away and don't use. Remove and set aside.

In a 4 qt. bowl or pot, mix the meat, salt and spices until well blended. Mix and knead with the water just until tacky and pliable enough to stuff the casings. Refrigerate until ready to fill the casings. (See Cook's Notes.)

With a sausage attachment on your stand mixer or by hand with a sausage funnel: Slide the casing, shirring it onto the end of it. Then pull about 2 inches off and tie the end into a knot. With the machine turned off, place the meat mix into the grinder. Turn on the machine and fill the casings with the meat until the whole casing is filled, being careful not to fill too tightly. Then proceed to twist each one a couple of times in the same direction at about 2 1/2 inches in length. Cut the links into groups of 4 or 6 sausages.

These sausages are like tiny breakfast links. Prepare by boiling or frying in a small amount of vegetable oil or on a barbeque grill. They are traditionally served on pita bread as a sandwich, but can certainly become a meat entrée.

Cook's Notes: Before filling the casings, cook a tablespoon of the mix in the microwave to taste the seasonings before making the sausages.

See "Where To Buy It" for online suppliers of sausage casings. Butcher shops can also supply them.

Sitto would tie them in twin rows, two by two, and cut them into groups of 4 or 6 for convenient handling. When ready to cook, even with the cut ends, the meat would firm up and not escape the casings.

When Elaine and I were young, we had no idea these Syrian housewives went through all this in preparing a meal! At the time, my sister Elaine's best quote for this dish was, "You'd better be in a good mood before you start this!"

Today's appliances make life a lot easier when making these homemade sausages mixed with chickpeas and rice. After they've been simmered, the best way to eat them is to pan fry them to a crispy goodness.

MORE HOMEMADE SAUSAGES
SILMANAT

1	CONTAINER HOG CASINGS
	LEMON OR ORANGE PEELS
1/2	CUP FLOUR, OR MORE IF NEEDED
2	LBS. GROUND LAMB (NOT AS LEAN AND GROUND TWICE)
1 1/2	TEASPOONS DATAH SPICE, OR TO TASTE (SEE GLOSSARY)
2	TEASPOONS SALT, OR TO TASTE (DIVIDED USE)
1	CUP COLD WATER
2	CUPS RICE, RAW
1	15 OZ. CAN CHICKPEAS (GARBANZO BEANS) DRAINED AND RINSED
1	TABLESPOON BAKING SODA
	CRISCO SHORTENING OR VEGETABLE OIL FOR FRYING

You will need 8 links of casings, about 8 to 12 inches long. After rinsing well, soak in cold water for several hours with lemon or orange rind. Rinse and discard the water.

Then, (and this is the incredible part) add some flour to your hands and rub the casing on the outside under running water. Then turn inside out under running water to clean out the insides of any residue. (See my sister's comment on this!)

Prepare the filling by combining the meat, spices and 1 teaspoon salt with the cup of water in a 4 qt. bowl to mix. Add the rice and chick peas and refrigerate until ready to fill the casings. (See Cook's Notes.)

Drain the casings and thread onto the mouth of a funnel or a KitchenAid sausage attachment, shirring until 2" or 3" remain hanging loosely. Knot the end. With the machine turned off, place the filling into it. Then turn on the machine and stuff the filling into the entire casing, being careful not to fill too tightly. Remove from the machine and then form the links by twisting the sausages a few times in the same direction at about 6" long for each one. Tie off the end to finish. The sausages will be larger and thicker than the previous recipe.

Put the sausages in a large 6 qt. pot, filled with water to cover and add 1 teaspoon salt and 1 tablespoon baking soda. Bring to a boil to soften the casings. Then lower to a simmer, uncovered. Skim the top to remove any sediment that rises. Pierce the sausages with a fork as they cook and simmer for 1 to 1 1/2 hours. Drain the sausages on paper towels and then fry in Crisco or vegetable oil until lightly browned on the outside. They may also be broiled, if desired.

Cook's Notes: Before filling the casings, cook a tablespoon of the mix in the microwave to taste the salt and seasonings. This will allow an adjustment before making the sausages.

Hog casings may be obtained as dried in salt, in a butcher shop or on-line. See "Where To Buy It" for a supplier.

Have you ever wished you could spend one more day with your grandmother? This happens to me a lot, especially when I am cooking or baking one of Sitto's old Syrian dishes. This meal is a fond reminder, as she made this dish often. Since the meat and vegetables bake in their sauce, it's an easy dish to bake on a busy day.

MEATLOAF WITH VEGETABLES
LAHMEH BIL FUHRUN

1	15 OZ. CAN TOMATO SAUCE
1/2	CUP WATER
1	TEASPOON LEMON JUICE
2	TABLESPOONS TAMARIND SYRUP (DIBIS)
1	TEASPOON SALT
2	WHITE POTATOES (THICKLY SLICED OR QUARTERED)
2	MEDIUM YELLOW ONIONS, QUARTERED
1	GREEN BELL PEPPER, SLICED
2	CARROTS, PEELED AND SLICED
1	CUP CAULIFLOWERETS
2	LBS. GROUND LAMB (GROUND ONCE)
2	TEASPOONS GROUND ALLSPICE
1	TEASPOON DATAH SPICE (SEE GLOSSARY)
2	TEASPOONS SALT

Meatloaf with Vegetables

Prepare the sauce:
In a 2-qt. saucepan, mix the tomato sauce, water, lemon juice, tamarind syrup and 1 teaspoon salt. Bring to a boil and lower to a simmer, for about 10 minutes.

Prepare the potatoes, onions, pepper, carrots, cauliflower and set aside.

Preheat oven to 350 degrees.

Mix the ground lamb, allspice, Datah spice and 2 teaspoons salt with moistened hands. Pat into an oiled 9" x 13" x 2" baking pan, to about 1" thick.

Place all of the vegetables over the meat in the pan. Pour the tomato sauce mixture over all and cover. Bake for 1 to 1 1/2 hours or until the vegetables are tender.

Slice the meat into squares, portion with the sauce and vegetables. Serve with cooked rice.

My sister and I loved our grandmother's version of this dish. However, in an effort to please my husband, I prepared my mother-in-law Mary's version of stuffed cabbage more often. Over time, I came to love her version as much as my grandmother's and her recipe follows. Mary used more of the tamarind syrup, lending a wonderful sweet-sour note to the dish. The slight differences in the amount of tomatoes and Tamarind syrup in these versions are an interesting take on the two generations!

SITTO NAIMA'S STUFFED CABBAGE
LAKHANA MALFUF MIN SITTO NAIMA

	2	**HEADS CABBAGE (WHOLE) RINSED**
Filling:		
	2	**CUPS RICE, RAW, RINSED AND DRAINED**
	2	**TABLESPOONS GROUND ALLSPICE**
	1	**LB. GROUND LAMB OR BEEF TABLESPOON**
	1	**SALT**
	2	**TABLESPOONS TOMATO PASTE**
	2	**CUPS WATER**
Spice Paste:		
	6	**CLOVES FRESH GARLIC**
	2	**TABLESPOONS DRIED PEPPERMINT FLAKES**
	1	**TABLESPOON SALT**
Cooking Liquid:		
	1/4 - 1/2	**CUP TAMARIND SYRUP (SEE BASICS)**
	1	**CUP LEMON JUICE, MORE OR LESS TO TASTE**
		WATER (SEE COOK'S NOTES)

Slit the core of the cabbage all around with 4 cuts, about 2 inches deep. This will facilitate the leaves' removal while simmering.

Parboil the cabbages, one at a time: Fill a 6 qt. pot halfway with water and bring to a boil. Place the cabbage into the pot and simmer just until the leaves soften somewhat, just blanching them about 1 minute per leaf. Remove the leaves one-by-one with tongs. Place on a platter to drain and cool.

Filling: In a 3 qt. bowl, mix the rice, allspice, meat, salt, tomato paste and water to make the filling. Set aside.

Spice Paste: In a mortar and pestle, crush the garlic, peppermint and salt and set aside. If you prefer a garlic press, use that and then add the mint flakes and salt to it while pressing with a fork to form a paste. Set aside.

To roll the cabbage leaves: Take each cabbage leaf, cutting out any tough portion of the leaf, which is near the core. Place about 2 to 3 tablespoons of the meat filling across the leaf, along the core side. Tuck in the ends and roll the cabbage. Put enough filling in the leaf to roll the size of a large, fat cigar. The amount will vary depending on the size of the leaf.

Put the filled cabbages into a 6 or 7 qt. stock pot, arranging in a pinwheel fashion, like spokes in a wheel. Add half the spice paste on this first layer. Then continue with the second and third layer of rolled cabbage, adding more spice paste to each layer.

Fill the pot with just enough water to cover the top layer. Add the lemon juice and tamarind syrup (Dibis). Place a plate over the cabbage rolls to keep the cabbages from moving while simmering. Cover the pot with a lid. Bring to a boil and then lower to a simmer, and cook for 45 minutes to one hour.

Cook's Notes: Taste the liquid at mid point to adjust for salt, lemon juice or more tamarind syrup, if desired.

Drain any liquid in the pot and reserve. Remove the cabbages and serve with reserved liquid as an added sauce on them, if desired. The rest of the liquid can be used to reheat the stuffed cabbages.

To prepare Mary's version, use this ratio and proceed as above:

MARY JWEID'S STUFFED CABBAGE
LAKHANA MALFUF MIN MARY JWEID

	2	**HEADS CABBAGE, RINSED**

Filling:

	2	**CUPS RICE, RAW, RINSED AND DRAINED**
	1 1/2	**LBS. GROUND LAMB OR BEEF**
	2	**TABLESPOONS GROUND ALLSPICE**
	1	**TABLESPOON SALT**
	1	**16 OZ. CAN TOMATOES, CRUSHED**
	1/4	**CUP WATER**

Spice Paste:

	6	**CLOVES FRESH GARLIC**
	2	**TABLESPOONS DRIED PEPPERMINT FLAKES**
	1	**TEASPOON SALT**

Cooking Liquid:

	1/2 - 3/4	**CUP TAMARIND SYRUP, OR TO TASTE (SEE BASICS)**
	3/4	**CUP LEMON JUICE**
		WATER (ENOUGH TO COVER THE TOP LAYER OF CABBAGES)

Mary Jweid's Stuffed Cabbage

Open Meat Pies

I was a teenager, about 13 or 14, when Uncle Antoun arrived from Syria. He was the last of our family to arrive. The entire family had saved for his ticket and it was a great accomplishment to finally have the whole family on this soil. Uncle Antoun was about 40 years old at the time and pretty set in his ways. He found America puzzling and kept comparing it to the "old country" in pretty unfavorable terms.

He stayed with my grandmother during this time. Sitto proudly served him the dishes of Aleppo, dishes that he knew so well, and which, as I've mentioned many times before, she was expert in preparing. You can imagine my shock one day, as we sat enjoying the open meat pies, Laham Ajin, one of my all time favorites. He began to rant and rave about how disappointing the meat pies were. "Mafi zait...Mafi semna...Mafi tami!" "No oil...no lard...no taste!" "These should be dripping with fat," he said. "These are too lean, they're tasteless!" I remember that my grandmother was very hurt at his remarks. As I listened, I couldn't believe his bad judgement, considering how great a cook she was.

It's only now that I realize that even an ethnic recipe that is painstakingly followed will be forever changed by the local availability of some items. In this case, the availability of leaner meats in this country compared with the meats of Aleppo, was a big factor. The individuality of the cook, with the nuances and liberties that might be taken with a dish over time, make it so much more the cook's "version." I can't help but wonder how many more dishes have become "leaner" with time and translation?

By the way, Uncle Antoun didn't last here very long. He was back home within the year, a combination of complaints and ungrateful attitude made it a lot easier to buy his ticket back to Aleppo, Syria.

OPEN MEAT PIES
LAHEM AJIN

1	PACKAGE DRY YEAST
	PINCH SUGAR
2	CUPS WARM WATER (DIVIDED USE)
3	TABLESPOONS CRISCO SHORTENING, MELTED
8	CUPS ALL PURPOSE FLOUR
1	TABLESPOON SALT
	ADDITIONAL FLOUR, AS NEEDED
1	TABLESPOON CRISCO SHORTENING, FOR GREASING BOWL

Dissolve the yeast in 1 cup of the warm water with the sugar, mix and set aside for 5 minutes until bubbly. Then add 3 tablespoons of the melted Crisco shortening.

Pour the flour into a large 6 qt. pot, add the salt and mix in to blend. Leave a well in the center and then add the yeast mixture into the flour well and mix. Continue with the rest of the water while gradually beginning to knead. You may need to add up to an additional cup of flour, if the dough is still sticky. Knead for about 10 to 15 minutes on a floured board until the dough appears to be smooth and elastic.

Coat the bottom of the pot with the tablespoon of Crisco shortening. Return the dough into the pot, turning the dough over to coat the top with the shortening. Cover and leave in a warm and draft-free area to rise, about 2 hours, until doubled in bulk. (I use my cold oven with the light on.)

Meat Topping:

1 1/2	TABLESPOONS SALT
2	TABLESPOONS GROUND ALLSPICE
2	TABLESPOONS DRY PEPPERMINT LEAVES, CRUMBLED
1	6 OZ. CAN TOMATO PASTE
3/4	CUP WATER
2	TABLESPOONS LEMON JUICE
1	CUP TAMARIND SYRUP (SEE BASICS)
2	LBS. LEAN GROUND LAMB OR BEEF
4	CUPS CHOPPED YELLOW ONIONS
1/4	LB. CRISCO SHORTENING

In a small cup, mix the salt, allspice and peppermint flakes together to blend and set aside.

In a 4 qt. bowl, mix the tomato paste, water, lemon juice and tamarind syrup and add the meat and blend well. Mix in the dry spices and then the chopped onions. Cover and chill until ready to use.

When the dough has risen to double its size, proceed with floured hands to pinch off 2" diameter size pieces and place on a floured cloth or wax paper to rest for about 15 to 30 minutes. Cover with a baking cloth, clean kitchen towel or wax paper. This allows the dough to rise a second time. They will rise to the approximate size of tennis balls.

Preheat the oven to 450 degrees.

Prepare the baking sheet by covering with aluminum foil and then rubbing about a tablespoon of Crisco vegetable shortening onto the foil.

Take each dough ball onto the baking sheet and flatten with your fingers into a circle, about 8" in diameter and about 1/8" to 1/4" thick, depending on your preference. With your fingers, spread about 3 to 4 tablespoons of the meat mixture onto each circle of dough. The meat should be spread thinly and evenly, to about 1/4" from the edge of the dough.

Bake the pies for 10 to 15 minutes. They will be sizzling and browned along the edges and the bottom when ready. Serve them hot or cool and refrigerate any leftovers or freeze in baggies for quick meals.

This recipe makes about 25 to 30 meat pies, depending on the size.

Cook's Notes: I line my baking sheets with foil for each new batch. It's easier than cleaning the baking sheets between batches, as some of the tamarind syrup tends to cook onto the sheets.

Open Meat Pies

Kibbe Nai is the foundation of many Syrian dishes. It is the star of the Mezze table and, without fail, can be found in many Arab households. Today's more sophisticated taste would consider it a Lamb Tartar. As a youngster, I enjoyed it with Syrian bread but the grownups would often add the scallions as a tasty nibble with the meat paste.

LAMB TARTAR
KIBBE NAI

2/3	CUP BULGAR WHEAT (#1 FINE GRAIN ONLY)
1	MEDIUM YELLOW ONION
1	TEASPOON SALT, OR TO TASTE
1 1/4	LBS. GROUND LAMB (LEG ONLY, LEAN AND GROUND TWICE)
	OLIVE OIL, PARSLEY, PAPRIKA, SCALLIONS FOR GARNISH

One hour before preparing the recipe, pour the wheat into a small bowl and add cold water to cover. Rinse the wheat a few times through a strainer and return to the bowl until ready to use.

Grate the onion.

Prepare a small bowl of ice water for working the mixture with your hands.

Use a 3 qt. bowl and combine the grated onion, salt and ground lamb. Squeeze out any moisture still in the wheat and then add it to the meat mixture. Using the ice water on your hands, knead the mixture into a smooth paste. Chill the meat before serving.

To finish Kibbe Nai and to serve as an appetizer for the Mezze Table:

On a decorative platter, plate the meat about an inch thick. Add a drizzle of olive oil, parsley or paprika and a few scallions for garnish. Serve raw with Syrian bread.

Cook's Notes: The ground lamb for this dish is of the highest quality, very lean, ground twice, from a trusted source. Middle Eastern butchers are the best source.

Bulgar wheat is available in three sizes: 1, 2 and 3, and is available at Middle Eastern stores. Only the fine #1 grind should be used in this recipe.

Lamb Tartar

Aleppo Lamb Meatballs

As an accomplished Aleppo cook, my grandmother would pride herself on both her Kibbe and her ability to make it perfectly. A thin meat shell, with no holes, enclosing the fragrant filling or Hashweh, would be the aim of all of these wonderful Syrian cooks.

The meat filling for traditional Aleppo lamb meatballs was as individual as the women who made them. Although the Aleppian stuffed Kibbe were known throughout Syria and the Middle East, each cook made the filling her own way. I feel that my grandmother's was moist and tastier because of the tamarind syrup she used in her version. After piercing the Kibbe with a fork, you had no doubt that a good Aleppo cook had made them!

I love the fact that the ground meat combined with the ice watered-hands make this an easy task to accomplish. I feel certain you'll be thrilled and proud of your ability in making these after trying them.

ALEPPO LAMB MEATBALLS
KIBBE HALABY MITLI

3/4	CUP BULGAR WHEAT (#1 FINE GRAIN)
1	MEDIUM YELLOW ONION, GRATED
1 1/2	TEASPOONS SALT, OR TO TASTE
1 1/2	LBS. GROUND LAMB (LEG ONLY, LEAN AND GROUND TWICE)
	OIL OR CRISCO SHORTENING FOR FRYING
1/2	CUP CLARIFIED BUTTER, BASICS, PAGE 7 (OPTIONAL)

Rinse the wheat in cold water a few times through a strainer. Drain the wheat and set aside in a small bowl until ready to use.

Prepare a small bowl of ice water for working the meat mixture with your hands.

Use a 4 qt. bowl and combine the grated onion, salt and ground lamb. Squeeze out any moisture in the wheat and then add it to the meat mixture, kneading it with ice-watered hands. Chill the meat until the filling is prepared.

MEAT FILLING
KIBBE HASHWEH

1/2	LB. GROUND LAMB (COARSELY GROUND)
1	MEDIUM YELLOW ONION, CHOPPED
1	TEASPOON SALT
1	TEASPOON GROUND ALLSPICE, OR MORE TO TASTE
1/4	CUP TAMARIND SYRUP, OR MORE TO TASTE (SEE BASICS)
1/4	CUP PINE NUTS OR COARSELY CHOPPED WALNUTS

In a 3 qt. bowl, mix the meat, salt and allspice to blend.

In a large 12" non-stick frying pan, spray the skillet lightly with cooking spray. Sauté the onions until limp. Then add the meat and sauté until both are lightly browned. Remove from the heat and add the tamarind syrup and nuts and mix well. Set aside to cool before stuffing the Kibbe meatballs.

To stuff the Aleppo lamb meatballs: Take a lemon-sized portion of the meat in the palm of one hand. With the thumb of your other hand, make a center indentation, working the meatball around your palm to form a shell that will hold the filling. As you twirl the meatball in your hand, with your thumb forming the cavity, you'll find that the shell will get thinner and thinner. The shell should be about 1/4" thick. Fill the cavity with about 1 heaping tablespoon of the meat filling and then seal the shell, making sure that the filing is not peeking out. Shape both ends of the filled meatball with pointed ends, like a football. Chill the meatballs for about 30 or more minutes.

Pour the oil about an inch or two deep into a 12" fry pan and heat. Fry the Kibbe until browned on all sides.

Serve hot. The meatballs are often accompanied by yogurt or tahini dressing and Syrian bread for a light lunch or as a meat entrée accompanied by rice and vegetables for dinner.

Optional baking method: Preheat the oven to 400 degrees.
Melt the clarified butter in a 9" x 13" x 2" baking pan by placing in the preheated oven for a few minutes. Remove the pan and then take each meatball and roll in the butter to coat it. Bake the meatballs for 40 to 50 minutes until browned. At a mid point, turn them again to get the top basted and then return right side up.

Another filling option: Hard boil eggs as a substitute for the meat (Hashweh). Drain, shell and cool the eggs. Prepare the meatballs as above. Sprinkle a dash of salt and allspice inside the raw meat pocket. Insert each egg and seal. Simmer in salted water for about 8 to 10 minutes. Drain and serve warm or cold as an appetizer or lunch.

It's a tribute to these Syrian cooks that they've taken a humble, basic dish, like Kibbe and have been able to prepare and serve it in so many ways. In today's busy world, with working mothers, it makes even more sense to make the basic Kibbe and be able to pick the version of the dish that suits the time available on that particular day. This is another great variation of Kibbe.

BAKED STUFFED PAN MEATLOAF
KIBBE B' SANNIEYEH

1	LAMB TARTAR RECIPE (KIBBE NAI) - PAGE 89, DOUBLED - KEEP PORTIONS SEPARATE
1	MEAT FILLING RECIPE (KIBBE HASHWEH) - PAGE 91, DOUBLED
3/4	CUP CLARIFIED BUTTER OR MARGARINE, MELTED (DIVIDED USE)

Pour half of the butter to coat a rectangular 9" x 13" x 2" pan.

Pat one half of the Kibbe Nai mixture to cover the bottom of the pan to about 3/4 inch thick.

Add the meat filling (Kibbe Hashweh) as a topping to cover the meat in the entire pan. Then cover the filling with the remaining half of the Kibbe Nai mix, smoothing the top with moistened hands to seal the filling. Chill the meatloaf for one hour.

When you are ready to bake, preheat the oven to 350 degrees.

Remove the pan from the refrigerator. Cut the meatloaf by making diagonal cuts 2" apart across the pan. Then reverse direction of the diagonal cuts, again 2" apart, to form diamond shapes. Pour the remainder of the butter over all.

Bake for 35 to 45 minutes until cooked and lightly browned on top. Cut through again and serve one or two diamond portions as an entrée.

Cook's Notes: This is a hearty dinner entrée served with rice and/or vegetables or for lunch with a salad. I have successfully substituted lean ground beef for this recipe.

Baked Stuffed Pan Meatloaf

SITTO'S KITCHEN

Sitto made my sister's favorite dish often. I must say, it's a meal in itself and perfect for a winter evening. I should note that my mother remembers my grandmother making this dish with quince when she was a youngster. In my sister's and my time, carrots were the stars of this dish.

LAMB MEATBALL AND CARROT STEW
KIBBE JAZARRIYA

1	LB. LAMB NECK BONES
1	LAMB TARTAR RECIPE (KIBBE NAI) - PAGE 89
1 1/2	TEASPOONS DATAH SPICE (SEE GLOSSARY)
5 - 6	CLOVES GARLIC, CRUSHED
2	TEASPOONS DRIED PEPPERMINT FLAKES
1 1/2	TABLESPOONS SALT, OR TO TASTE (DIVIDED USE)
6	CARROTS, PEELED, CUT INTO THICK SLICES
1	LEMON, JUICED
1 - 2	TABLESPOONS SUGAR, TO TASTE
	DASH ALEPPO PEPPER OR BLACK PEPPER
2 - 4	TABLESPOONS TAMARIND SYRUP, TO TASTE (SEE BASICS)
	RICE, PREPARE PER PACKAGE

Rinse the lamb bones in cold water several times until the water runs clear. Place them in a 6 qt. pot, adding enough water to cover and bring to a boil. Lower the heat and skim as needed. Add 1 tablespoon of salt, cover and simmer 1-1/2 to 2 hours or until the meat is tender and can be pulled off the bones.

While the bones simmer, prepare the basic Kibbe Nai recipe and add the Datah spice to the mixture. Form into 1 1/2" meatballs. Refrigerate until needed.

In a mortar and pestle, mash the garlic, peppermint and 1/2 tablespoon of salt to a paste.

Remove the bones from the water, reserving the broth. Let them cool enough to clean the meat off the bones and place in a small bowl, discarding the bones.

Strain and skim any fat from the meat broth. Then add the meat pieces, carrots, lemon juice, sugar, garlic paste mixture, pepper and tamarind syrup to the broth. Simmer, covered about 20 minutes. Taste seasonings and adjust if needed.

Then add the Kibbe meatballs. Simmer for another 20 to 25 minutes or until the meat is cooked and well seasoned.

Serve with white rice.

Cook's Notes: Use 2 tablespoons of tamarind syrup at first and when adjusting for seasonings, add more tamarind, if preferred.

Lamb Meatball and Carrot Stew

93

My sister, Elaine, loves this dish and I can thank her for getting this recipe from Sitto, who made it often for her. It's a hearty dish that many consider comfort food.

LAMB MEATBALLS IN YOGURT
KIBBE LABANIYA

1	LAMB TARTAR RECIPE (KIBBE NAI) - PAGE 89
2	TEASPOONS DATAH SPICE (SEE GLOSSARY)
1/4	CUP SWEET OR CLARIFIED BUTTER, CHILLED
1/2	CUP COLD WATER
2	TEASPOONS CORNSTARCH (DIVIDED USE)
2	QTS. HOMEMADE YOGURT OR COMMERCIAL, PLAIN
2	TEASPOONS SALT (DIVIDED USE)
1	CUP RICE, COOKED
1 - 2	TABLESPOONS FRESH PEPPERMINT FLAKES, CHOPPED

Prepare the lamb tartar (Kibbe Nai) recipe with the addition of the Datah spice and 1 teaspoon salt to the mix. Make small 1" balls, placing a bit of butter inside each meatball. Set aside.

Mix 1 teaspoon of cornstarch into the half cup of cold water to thoroughly blend. (See Cook's Notes.)

Place the yogurt into a large 5 qt. pot and add the blended cornstarch and add the other teaspoon of salt.

Heat the yogurt, slowly, stirring constantly in the same direction, until the mixture boils. Then add the rice and lower to a simmer. Add the Kibbe meatballs, cover and continue to simmer until the meatballs are cooked, approximately 45 to 60 minutes.

Serve in bowls with a sprinkling of mint.

Cook's Notes: If the yogurt is too thin, add the additional teaspoon of cornstarch in a small amount of cold water to blend. Then add to the simmering yogurt to thicken it further.

Lamb Meatballs in Yogurt

As a youngster, I remember we would all look forward to the Maharajans. These summer church festivals were always in park settings, with every family bringing their favorite picnic foods and grills.

Years later my children also loved the grilled Kibbe that Sitto made. I do remember that this meat mixture was pressed around a skewer to form a sausage shape or sometimes served as a patty. It was simple and delicious served with potato salad and Syrian bread.

GROUND LAMB ON A SKEWER
KIBBE AL'SIKH

1/2	CUP BULGAR WHEAT (#1 FINE GRAIN)
1 1/4	LBS. GROUND LAMB
1	TEASPOON SALT, OR TO TASTE
1	ONION, GRATED FINE
1/4	CUP FRESH PEPPERMINT LEAVES, CHOPPED

Pour the Bulgar into a 1 qt. bowl. Cover in cold water and set aside for 1 hour.

In a 3 qt. bowl, mix the meat with the salt, onion and peppermint to blend.

Drain the Bulgar by pouring it through a strainer. Squeeze it to remove most of the moisture and then add it to the meat mixture.

Prepare a small bowl of ice water to wet your hands as you knead the meat mixture. This will help shape the meat around skewers.

Press the meat around the skewers to form a sausage shape. Grill the skewers on the barbeque or under the broiler.

To serve the skewers: Diners can unthread the Kibbe by wrapping Syrian bread around the meat. Any salad completes the feast!

Cook's Notes: I have used dried mint flakes, about a tablespoon, when I have not had the fresh mint available to me.

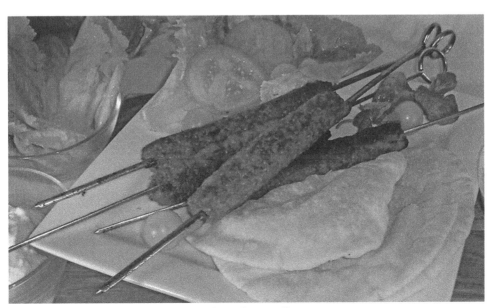

Ground Lamb on a Skewer

My sister, Elaine, has perfected this recipe of our grandmother's and serves it often. It's a really easy dish, even with the artichoke preparation. In those days, it was always special as artichokes had a short season.

LAMB AND ARTICHOKES
SHOKE W' LAHMEH

1	LEMON CUT IN HALF (DIVIDED USE)
7 - 8	FRESH ARTICHOKES
1	LB. GROUND LAMB (GROUND ONCE)
1	TABLESPOON GROUND ALLSPICE
2	TEASPOONS SALT (DIVIDED USE)
2	MEDIUM YELLOW ONIONS, CHOPPED
1	TABLESPOON OLIVE OIL
	RICE, PREPARE PER PACKAGE

Lamb and Artichokes

Prepare acidulated water for the artichoke soak:
Fill a 3 qt. bowl halfway with cold water and the juice of 1/2 of the lemon. Drop in the lemon half, as well, and set aside.

Prepare the artichoke:
Wash the artichoke under running water. Cut off the stem to about 1" with a sharp paring knife. Peel the stem end and tear off and discard the large outer leaves. With a scissor, cut off the tips of the remaining inner more tender leaves to remove the thorns.

Then cut the artichoke in half lengthwise. Clean out the pinkish prickly center with a sharp, pointed knife and also clean out the fuzzy choke carefully to remove it all and discard. Take care not to cut into the meaty heart. Cut the artichoke again into fourths. Immediately drop the artichoke segments into the acidulated water to soak while preparing the rest. This soak will prevent discoloration.

Rinse the artichokes to clean well and place in a 4 qt. covered saucepan. Add enough fresh water to cover, along with the juice of the remaining lemon half and the teaspoon of salt. Bring to a boil and then simmer until the hearts are just fork tender.

While the artichokes are simmering, mix the lamb, allspice, and salt in a 2 qt. bowl.

In a non-stick 12" skillet, sauté the lamb mixture with the chopped onions in olive oil until cooked. Add the cooked and drained artichoke and stir. Simmer for a few more minutes to blend the flavors. Serve over rice.

Starting a grapevine was an important part of the basic Arab kitchen and every one of our family members and Syrian friends planted one. I can remember my uncle George cutting off a root and offering it to one of my cousins.

Throughout those summers of my youth, my grandmother would pick the top newer leaves off her grapevine. The lighter, tender green leaves were all that she'd choose. I watched as they were wrapped in stacks of 20, the shiny side facing up, rolled and wound with string. She would then drop them in boiling water to blanch them for just a few minutes until they turned a brownish green color. She'd rinse them in cold water and drain them, squeezing them gently. She'd place them to soak in her large pottery jars filled with her brine and our family would have stuffed grape leaves all year round.

Years later, as more modern methods began to take hold in her kitchen, she'd pick the leaves, rinse them, tie them into packets of 20, and drop them in boiling water to blanch for a few minutes. She'd squeeze out the water and place the packets of leaves in plastic bags to freeze and use as needed.

Stuffed cold grape leaves are found throughout the Middle East as a Mezze dish. However, the Aleppo cooks never served this dish cold and cherished it as a hot entrée.

Nowadays, unless you have a grapevine, it's harder getting fresh grape leaves. Preserved commercial grape leaves in jars can be used. See the cook's notes for details.

STUFFED GRAPE LEAVES
YEBRET

2	CUPS RICE, RAW
3	TABLESPOONS GROUND ALLSPICE, OR MORE TO TASTE
1	TABLESPOON TOMATO PASTE (HEAPING)
1 1/2	TEASPOONS SALT
2	LBS. GROUND LAMB, GROUND ONCE OR GROUND BEEF
2 1/2	CUPS WATER (DIVIDED USE)
3/4	LB. GRAPE LEAVES, TIED IN BUNDLES & PARBOILED IF FRESH (ABOUT 60-70)
2	CUPS LEMON JUICE, OR TO TASTE
1 1/2	HEADS OF GARLIC, PEELED (DIVIDED USE)

Soak the rice in a 3 qt. bowl of cold water to cover for 30 minutes. After rinsing the rice once or twice, add the allspice into it, mixing until the rice turns brown. Then add the tomato paste, salt, ground meat and 1/2 cup of the water and blend all with your hands. Set aside or chill until ready to fill the leaves.

If using fresh grape leaves, parboil in a 2 qt. saucepan for 1 to 2 minutes, squeeze to drain and cool. Remove any stems from the ends of the leaves.

To stuff a grape leaf: Place the leaf with the vein side up facing you, and the stem side closest to you. Place a cigar-shaped amount of filling across the leaf but not end to end. Then turn in the left and right sides of the leaf and begin rolling away from you, keeping the filling firmly in place as you finish rolling. Place on a platter while you work. Keep track of rolled leaves which are larger and reserve them for the bottom of the pot.

Place the rolled grape leaves in a large 5 or 6 qt. pot, spiral row fashion, with cloves of whole garlic in between each row, reserving 8 cloves for the cooking liquid spices below.

Mix the remaining 2 cups of water and lemon juice and pour over all the rolled grape leaves in the pot. Bring to a boil while you prepare the spices.

Spices for the cooking liquid:

8	**GARLIC CLOVES**
1	**TEASPOON SALT**
1	**TEASPOON PEPPERMINT FLAKES**

Combine the garlic, salt and peppermint flakes and pound together in a mortar and pestle or a food processor to make a paste. Put the paste into the liquid portion of the pot. Cover with a heavy plate and the pot lid and lower to a simmer for 45 minutes until cooked.

At a mid point in the simmer, taste the liquid and adjust the lemon water and seasoning. If you find that the liquid has been absorbed, you may add more lemon juice and water in equal amounts at this point. Test one roll from the top center for doneness.

Using tongs, place the stuffed grape leaves on a platter. Pour out the liquid into a gravy boat or pitcher to serve with the grape leaves. Most servings are for approximately 8 to 10 per person.

Cook's Notes: My sister has doubled the allspice and tomato paste, increased the water and decreased the lemon juice with delicious results, again proving each cook's individuality!

Use two 16 oz. jars of commercial grape leaves if fresh leaves are unavailable. To prepare: Pour out the liquid and place the leaves in a large bowl. Rinse the leaves 5 times in cold water and let them soak in clear, cold water to cover for 1/2 hour. Fill a large pot half-way with water and bring to a boil. Place the drained leaves into the water. Turn off the heat immediately and steep for only 2 minutes and drain into a colander. Run cold water over the leaves, squeeze dry and proceed as above to fill with the meat mixture.

Stuffed Grape Leaves

Sitto's Stuffed Squash

The Syrian cook who could successfully core the squash almost to its shell without piercing it would surely be considered a seasoned cook. It took me many tries before I could present a shell without a hole in it! I really worked on it since Mahshi was my favorite dish. Two versions follow, my grandmother's and my mother-in-law Mary's.

SITTO'S STUFFED SQUASH
KUSA MAHSHI MIN SITTO

1	**CUP RICE, RAW**
1	**TABLESPOON GROUND ALLSPICE**
1/2	**TEASPOON SALT**
1/4	**CUP TOMATO PASTE**
1/2	**LB. GROUND LAMB OR BEEF**
1/4	**CUP WATER**
6	**CLOVES GARLIC, PEELED**
1	**TEASPOON SALT**
1	**TEASPOON DRIED PEPPERMINT FLAKES**
6	**GREEN OR YELLOW SQUASH (EITHER OR BOTH)**
1 - 2	**TABLESPOONS TAMARIND SYRUP (SEE BASICS)**
1/2	**CUP LEMON JUICE**

Prepare the filling:
In a 3 qt. bowl, soak the rice in water for 30 minutes. Rinse and drain the water from the rice. Mix in the allspice, 1/2 teaspoon salt and tomato paste. Then add the ground meat with the 1/4 cup of water to blend well. Refrigerate until ready to fill the squash.

Preparing the Squash

Pound the garlic, teaspoon of salt and peppermint in a mortar and pestle to a paste. Or use a garlic press, combine and set aside.

Prepare the squash:
Slice the top stems off the squash. Then, use a corer to remove the fleshy center of the squash. Do this repeatedly until you've reached bottom - being careful not to pierce the skin. Continue to "clean out" the insides of the squash until the shell thickness is about 1/4" thick.

With the tines of the fork, scrape the outside of the squash from top to bottom, making vertical lines along the outside of the shell. Rinse out and then fill the squash with the meat filling up to 1/2" from the top of the squash.

Layer the squash in a large 6 qt. pot. Pour enough water over the squash to just below the top layer. Add the tamarind syrup to the liquid. Then add the garlic paste to the lemon juice and pour all around the squash. Cover the squash with a heavy plate to keep it from floating during cooking. Cover the pot and bring to a boil. Then lower to a simmer for about 45 minutes to an hour. Taste at the mid-point to adjust seasonings. More tamarind, lemon or water may be added per individual taste.

Cook's Notes: The implements the Syrian cook has used for coring the squash were initially handmade. My mother-in-law gave me a set she had. It consisted of a tubular piece of steel, about 1" in diameter by 6" long. The other tool looks like a longer, slimmer version of a 2-sided apple corer, with one side smaller than the other. These implements can now be obtained at Middle Eastern stores. See the photo in "Stocking the Syrian Cook's Kitchen."

My grandmother always saved the leftover squash pulp and she prepared it as stewed squash with herbs and onions.

My mother-in-law's recipe for stuffed squash uses no lemon juice and quite a bit more of the Tamarind syrup, which she called Dibis. She always cooked for a crowd and we all loved the leftovers. This amount of squash was typical for her. You could halve the recipe quite successfully, if you prefer.

MARY'S STUFFED SQUASH
KUSA MAHSHI MIN MARY

16	SQUASH, GREEN AND YELLOW
2	CUPS RICE, RAW
3	TABLESPOONS GROUND ALLSPICE
1	TABLESPOON SALT
1/2	TEASPOON PEPPER
1	28 OZ. CAN PLUM TOMATOES, CRUSHED
6	OZ. TOMATO PASTE
2 1/2	LBS. GROUND LAMB OR BEEF
6	OZ. WATER (APPROXIMATE)

Core the squash and remove the inside to about 1/4" thickness of the shell of the squash. (See the Cook's Notes for Sitto's Stuffed Squash.) Scrape the outside with the lines of a fork to make vertical ridges from the top down the length of the squash. Rinse the squash, drain and set aside.

Make the filling by first rinsing the rice in a measuring cup a few times. Drain the water out and pour into a 4 qt. bowl. Then add the allspice, salt and pepper, then the tomatoes and tomato paste. Add the meat with enough water to allow the filling mixture to be easily stuffed into the squash shells.

In a large 7 or 8 qt. pot, layer the stuffed squash in a circular fashion, overlapping layers as necessary. Set aside while you prepare the spices for the cooking liquid.

1	HEAD OF GARLIC, PEELED
1	TEASPOON SALT
4	TABLESPOONS DRIED PEPPERMINT FLAKES
1 1/2	CUPS TAMARIND SYRUP (SEE BASICS)

In a mortar and pestle or food processor, pulverize the garlic cloves, salt and peppermint flakes together to form a paste.

Pour water into the pot just below the top layer of squash, then add the tamarind syrup and the garlic paste, spooning it all around the squash.

Cover the squash with a heavy dish or bowl to keep the squash from floating. Cover the pan as well. Bring to a boil and then lower to a simmer for 50 minutes. Taste at a mid-point to adjust seasonings, if necessary. Test before serving to be sure the filling and squash are cooked.

Another remembrance I have of my grandmother was her use of mint to make her basic spice paste. She used it for stuffed grape leaves (Yebret), stuffed squash (Mahshi), and stuffed cabbage (Lakhana), among other dishes. She would take out her heavy, well-worn brass mortar and pestle, the Hehwaan. She'd pound the coarse salt and garlic until pureed, and then add the dried mint flakes to make a paste of these basic ingredients. In fact, all of her ground spices were to be pounded at one time or another in this old brass mortar and pestle brought from Aleppo. How I treasure it in my kitchen today!

Today, of course, when I'm rushed, I may use my garlic press or blender. But, I must say, the pounding in the mortar and pestle is by far a more authentic blending of the spices with the garlic and I know it infused her dishes and mine with a deeper, richer flavor.

SYRIAN STUFFED PEPPERS
MASHI FIL FUL SHAMI

For the filling:

4	**GREEN BELL PEPPERS, MEDIUM**
3/4	**CUP RICE (RAW)**
1	**TABLESPOON ALLSPICE**
1	**TEASPOON SALT**
1/2	**LB. GROUND LAMB OR BEEF**
2	**TABLESPOONS TOMATO PASTE (6 OZ. CAN – SAVE REMAINDER FOR SAUCE)**
1/4	**CUP DICED TOMATOES, CRUSHED (SAVE REMAINDER OF 14.5 OZ. CAN FOR SAUCE)**
1/4	**CUP WATER**

Syrian Stuffed Peppers

For the sauce:

1 1/3	**CUPS DICED TOMATOES, CRUSHED**
	REMAINDER OF TOMATO PASTE
2	**CUPS WATER**
1	**TEASPOON SALT**
3	**CLOVES GARLIC**
1	**TABLESPOON LEMON JUICE**
1	**TEASPOON PARSLEY, CHOPPED OR DRIED**
1/8	**TEASPOON ALEPPO PEPPER**
1	**TEASPOON DATAH SPICE (SEE GLOSSARY)**
1	**TEASPOON DRIED MINT FLAKES**
1	**TABLESPOON TAMARIND SYRUP**

Rinse the peppers and dry. Slice the tops off of the peppers and discard. Carefully remove the core and pith inside. Rinse to remove all seeds. Drain and dry.

Prepare the filling:
Rinse and drain the rice. In a large bowl, add 1 tablespoon allspice, 1 teaspoon salt, 2 tablespoons tomato paste, 1/4 cup of crushed tomatoes and 1/4 cup water. Then add the ground meat to this mixture and blend well.

Fill the green peppers with the meat mixture, leaving about 1/2 inch from the top. Press the top of the stuffing lightly, but do not pack down. The rice will open up as it cooks and this is why they should not be filled to the top. Refrigerate and make the sauce.

Prepare the sauce:
Mash the garlic and salt in a mortar and pestle, garlic press or blender. Pour the remainder of the diced tomatoes, tomato paste, water, salt and garlic paste, lemon juice, spices and tamarind into a 2 qt. saucepan. Simmer for about 30 minutes. Taste the seasonings and adjust to your liking.

Pour the sauce into a 5 qt. pot, reserving 1 cup. Layer the peppers upright in the pot. Spoon a few tablespoons of the reserved sauce over the filling. Cover and bring to a boil. Lower to a simmer for 1 to 1 1/2 hours, or until the peppers are tender and the rice is cooked.

Cook's Notes: I use a diffuser under the pot to avoid any scorching of the bottom of the peppers. Check to ensure the peppers are not sticking. They may be gently moved at a mid point to be sure.

The yogurt and lemon marinade makes for a very tender grilled chicken kabob. This can be made ahead and takes just minutes to grill. This is wonderful on any of the rice dishes or on warm Syrian bread.

GRILLED CHICKEN KABOBS
DJAAJ MISHWI KABOB

2	CHICKEN BREASTS, BONELESS/SKINLESS, RINSE AND DRY
2	CLOVES GARLIC
1/2	TEASPOON SALT, OR MORE TO TASTE
1	TABLESPOON CHOPPED FRESH PEPPERMINT OR 1 TEASPOON DRIED MINT
1	CUP YOGURT (HOMEMADE OR PLAIN COMMERCIAL BRAND)
2	TABLESPOONS LEMON JUICE
	DASH ALEPPO PEPPER
1	GREEN BELL PEPPER
1	RED OR YELLOW BELL PEPPER
1	SMALL YELLOW ONION
4	SKEWERS FOR GRILLING

Add a sheet of wax paper onto the top of a cutting board. Place the chicken on it and cover with a second piece of wax paper. Pound the breasts with a meat tenderizer or heavy pan to an even thickness. Then cut each breast into 2" square pieces. Set aside.

In a mortar and pestle, pound the garlic, salt and mint into a paste. If preferred, use a food processor or garlic press.

Combine the garlic paste with the yogurt, lemon juice and Aleppo Pepper in a 2 qt. bowl.

Coat the chicken pieces with the yogurt/garlic marinade and chill for at least an hour, preferably several hours.

Cut each pepper in half, removing seeds and stems. Rinse the peppers and dry. Cut each pepper again into quarters, then crosswise, making 8 pieces per pepper, approximately 1 1/2" square.

Peel the onion, cutting the top and bottom off. Then cut the onion in quarters, lengthwise. Then cut crosswise, to make 1 1/2" squares. Place the vegetables in a small bowl and set aside.

Preheat the grill.

Thread the skewers, alternating the chicken, green, red or yellow peppers and onion slices. Discard any remaining marinade.

Grill and serve over rice or in halved Syrian bread.

Cook's Notes: It's easier to thread the chicken on to flat skewers, like my grandmother's, since chicken can be slippery. If your skewers are round, you may prefer threading the chicken onto two skewers at a time to prevent slippage.

My mother-in-law Mary's Sunday chicken recipe was much loved. She always felt that garlic made the dish. I agree and would add that her homemade stock made it very special.

MARY'S CHICKEN WITH RICE AND TOMATOES
DJAAJ MA' RIZ W' BANADURA MIN MARY

1	CHICKEN 3 TO 4 LBS
3	TABLESPOONS SALT (DIVIDED USE)
1	28 OZ. CAN WHOLE PLUM TOMATOES
1	6 OZ. CAN TOMATO PASTE (USE HALF THE CAN)
1/2	CUP WATER
2	CLOVES OF GARLIC, SLIVERED
1/2	TEASPOON BLACK PEPPER
1/4	TEASPOON ALEPPO PEPPER OR RED PEPPER FLAKES
1	TEASPOON SUGAR
2	CUPS LONG GRAIN RICE (RAW)

Prepare the stock:
Wash the chicken, inside and out. Remove the neck, giblets and rinse.

In a large 7 qt. stockpot, place the whole fryer chicken, neck and giblets in water to cover. Bring to a boil and then simmer until tender, skimming any foam that rises to the surface. Add 2 tablespoons of salt when almost finished. Remove the chicken and place in a rectangular baking pan.

Strain the stock into a large 4 qt. bowl, reserving 2/3 cup of stock for the sauce (following) and 4 cups of stock for the rice preparation. Freeze or refrigerate any remaining stock for chicken or rice dishes.

Prepare the sauce for the chicken:
Place the plum tomatoes into a blender to lightly break them up. Pour the tomatoes into a 3 qt. saucepan. Add the half can of paste, 1/2 cup of water and 2/3 cup of reserved chicken stock from the stockpot. Then add the garlic, salt, black pepper, Aleppo or red pepper flakes and sugar. Simmer for 15 minutes and set aside.

Preheat the oven to 325 degrees.

Cover the chicken with the prepared sauce and bake uncovered for 1 hour, basting 3 or 4 times with the sauce during this time

In the last half hour while the chicken bakes, prepare the rice:
Pour the 4 cups reserved stock and 2 cups of rice into a 5 qt. pot. Stir the rice and the stock with a fork and bring to a boil. Then lower the heat, cover and simmer for 20 minutes or until fork tender.

Serve the baked chicken and rice along with the tomato sauce. Any vegetable or salad of your choice would be good accompaniments.

CHICKEN WITH LEMON
DJAAJ B' LAIMUN

4	**CHICKEN BREASTS, BONELESS AND SKINLESS**
1/2	**CUP FLOUR**
1/2	**TEASPOON SALT, OR TO TASTE**
1/4	**TEASPOON PEPPER**
4	**TABLESPOONS CLARIFIED BUTTER OR MARGARINE**
1/4	**CUP OLIVE OIL**
4	**GARLIC CLOVES, CRUSHED**
1	**LEMON, HALVED**

Cover a cutting board with a sheet of wax paper. Place the chicken breasts on it and add another piece of wax paper to cover them. Pound the breasts to an even thickness using a meat tenderizer or a heavy pan. Cut each breast in half, lengthwise.

Rinse and drain the chicken. Do not pat dry. Place in a 3 qt. bowl and set aside.

In a small 2 qt. bowl, blend the flour, salt and pepper. Dredge the moist chicken in the flour and place on a flat plate.

Heat the butter and olive oil in a large 12" sauté pan over medium heat. Add the crushed garlic, stirring quickly for a few seconds without browning it.

Then add the chicken, keeping the heat moderate to allow the chicken to cook to a golden brown. Then turn the chicken over and brown the other side. This should take about 4 to 5 minutes for each side.

When the chicken is golden, squeeze the two lemon halves over it.

Place the chicken on a platter and drizzle the garlic-lemon pan scrapings over all.

Serve alongside Rice with Noodles, Rice Pilaf or any other side dish.

Cook's Notes: This recipe will work for fish filets, as well. If making the fish, you may wish to eliminate the garlic and squeeze the lemon over all. Finish with chopped, fresh parsley.

Years ago, Uncle Nickie and Aunt Carmie introduced us to this wonderful grilled Herb Chicken and it's been a frequent entrée on our family grills all summer long ever since.

GRILLED HERBED CHICKEN
DJAAJ MISHWI

3	**CLOVES GARLIC**
1/2	**TEASPOON SALT**
1/2	**CUP OLIVE OIL**
4	**TABLESPOONS BUTTER (CLARIFIED IS PREFERRED)**
1	**TABLESPOON CHOPPED FRESH THYME**
1	**TABLESPOON CHOPPED PARSLEY**
1/2	**CUP LEMON JUICE**
	DASH PEPPER
4	**CHICKEN BREASTS, BONELESS, SKINLESS**
5 - 6	**SPRIGS FRESH THYME WITH STEMS TIED TOGETHER**

Pound the garlic cloves and salt in a mortar and pestle or use a garlic press and blend in the salt to make a paste.

Place the olive oil, butter, garlic paste, chopped thyme, parsley, lemon juice and pepper into a 1 qt. saucepan. Simmer for about 5 minutes. Set aside to cool.

Reserve about 1/4 cup of the marinade. Pour the rest of the cooled marinade over the chicken breasts to marinate in the refrigerator for an hour or more.

Tie the stems of the fresh thyme together with string around the end of a long-handled wooden spoon to form a "basting brush." Place the tied fresh thyme into the 1/4 cup of reserved marinade for basting the chicken on the grill and set aside.

Heat the barbeque grill or broiler if using the oven.

Remove the chicken from the bowl, discarding the soaking marinade.

Grill the chicken breasts over medium heat. At a mid point, begin to brush the reserved 1/4 cup of marinade with the thyme "basting brush" over the chicken until cooked and nicely grilled.

Cook's Notes: The original recipe used bone-in chicken breasts. The chicken can be grilled this way but use a lower flame and grill longer to ensure the chicken cooks through and before basting with the reserved marinade to finish grilling.

I've also used fresh oregano instead of the thyme.

I remember Sitto's kitchen had a simple white enamel stovetop oven. As if it were yesterday, I can see her pulling out that small broiling drawer to reveal this hot baked macaroni supper dish. We all loved the browned topping on the pasta, especially my Mom, who always liked it toasty brown...giving it that crunch that I can still remember!

BAKED MEATY MACARONI
MACAROONEH W' LAHMEH BIL FUHRUN

Sauce:

1	15 OZ. CAN TOMATO SAUCE
1	15 OZ. CAN DICED TOMATOES
2	CUPS WATER
1 1/2	TEASPOONS SALT, OR TO TASTE
1	CLOVE GARLIC, MINCED, OR MORE TO TASTE TEASPOON LEMON
1	JUICE, FRESH
1	TABLESPOON TAMARIND SYRUP
2	TABLESPOONS FRESH PARSLEY LEAVES, CHOPPED
	DASH ALEPPO PEPPER

Meat:

3/4	LB. GROUND LAMB
1/2	TEASPOON SALT, OR TO TASTE
1	TABLESPOON DATAH SPICE (SEE GLOSSARY)
1	MEDIUM YELLOW ONION, DICED
1	TABLESPOON OLIVE OIL

Pasta:

12	OZ. LARGE MACARONI, PENNE, ROTINI, ELBOW OR OTHER
1/2	TEASPOON SALT

Oil a 9" x 13" baking or casserole pan and set aside.

To make the sauce, combine the tomatoes, water, salt, garlic, lemon juice, tamarind, parsley and Aleppo Pepper in a 3 qt. saucepan and simmer for 25 to 30 minutes. Keep on a very low heat.

Mix the meat, salt and spice together and set aside.

Heat the olive oil in a 12" fry pan and sauté the onion until cooked and golden. Remove with a slotted spoon and add the onions to the simmering sauce.

Sauté the meat in the same fry pan until browned. Drain on paper toweling and then add it to the sauce.

Preheat the oven to 375 degrees.

Boil the macaroni in salted water until tender, per package directions. Drain and spoon into the baking pan.

Pour the meat sauce over the macaroni in the baking pan, reserving any sauce for serving, if preferred.

Bake for 10 minutes.

Finish by broiling the top of the casserole until the macaroni is browned and crunchy.

Cook's Notes: If you prefer the pasta without broiling, serve after baking. Beef may be substituted for the ground lamb.

VEGETABLES

I remember shopping for produce with my grandmother and noting that she always concentrated on the vegetables first, only choosing what was in season. She'd often show me how to pick the vegetables or ripe fruit and how to judge them for freshness. When I was young, she'd sometimes laugh at my selections and later, I'd be so proud when she'd accept my choice.

SPINACH WITH LENTILS
SBANIKH MA' ADDES

3/4	CUP LENTILS, LARGE BROWN
3	CUPS WATER
1	LB. FRESH SPINACH
1	MEDIUM YELLOW ONION, CHOPPED
4	TABLESPOONS OLIVE OIL
4	GARLIC CLOVES, CRUSHED
1	TEASPOON GROUND CORIANDER
1	TEASPOON GROUND CUMIN
1	TEASPOON SALT
	BLACK PEPPER, TO TASTE
	LEMON HALF

Sort the lentils in a small bowl, removing any stones or broken lentils. Rinse and drain.

In a 3 qt. saucepan, add the lentils and water. Bring to a boil, covered, and lower to a simmer for about 20 to 30 minutes or until tender. Lentils may vary in cooking time.

Remove the stems from the spinach leaves, wash well, and drain.

In a large 12" skillet, sauté the onion in the olive oil, until golden. Then add the garlic and sauté just for a minute or two. Set aside.

Drain the cooked lentils, reserving 1/2 cup of the liquid.

Add the fresh spinach and the reserved lentil liquid to the onions in the skillet. Then add the fresh ground coriander and cumin, salt and pepper. Sauté for a few minutes until the spinach is wilted and cooked. Add the lentils, stirring over the heat until the dish is well mixed. Taste the seasonings and adjust.

Spoon the spinach and lentils into a serving dish. To finish, squeeze a lemon half over all for a fresh taste.

Cook's Notes: I use whole spices in my spice grinder for the best flavor.

Who doesn't remember their grandmother stringing beans? It was always a good time to sit at the kitchen table with Sitto and help prepare the beans as we talked about things.

STRING BEANS WITH MEAT AND TOMATOES
FOWLEH MA' LAHEM W' BANADURA

1	MEDIUM YELLOW ONION
1/2	LB. GROUND LAMB (COARSELY GROUND) OR BEEF
1	TEASPOON SALT
1	TEASPOON GROUND ALLSPICE
1/4	CUP OLIVE OIL
1	CLOVE GARLIC, CHOPPED (OPTIONAL)
1	8 OZ. CAN TOMATO SAUCE
	DASH ALEPPO PEPPER, OR TO TASTE
1	LB. FRESH STRING BEANS, STRINGS REMOVED, ENDS CUT, RINSED
1	CUP OF WATER
	RICE, COOKED ACCORDING TO PACKAGE

String Beans With Meat and Tomatoes

Chop the onion and set aside.

Mix the meat, salt and allspice in a 2 qt. bowl to blend.

In a large 12" skillet or frying pan, sauté the meat and onion in the olive oil until the onions and meat are lightly browned. Add the chopped garlic to this sauté, if using. Then add the tomato sauce. Sprinkle with the Aleppo Pepper and then remove from the heat and set aside.

Place the prepared string beans in a 5 qt. Dutch oven or pot along with the cup of water. Bring to a boil and lower the heat to a simmer. Then add the sautéed meat mixture to the string beans and mix. Cover the pot and simmer for about 30 minutes. Taste the seasonings and adjust if necessary.

Remove from the heat when the beans are tender and serve over cooked rice.

When planning our meals, Sitto concentrated on the vegetables first, always choosing what was fresh and in season. Today's cooks can choose from year-round produce selections and have no concern for seasonal cooking. Squash is a perfect example of this. And the great part about stewed vegetables is that the cook can be liberal in choosing any favorite vegetables and herbs. These Aleppo seasonings make every version special.

STEWED SQUASH
KUSA MATBUKH

3	YELLOW OR GREEN SQUASH (OR BOTH) YELLOW
2	ONIONS, MEDIUM, LARGE DICE
2	RED POTATOES, CUBED
3	CLOVES GARLIC, MINCED OR CRUSHED
4	RIPE TOMATOES
1	15 OZ. CAN TOMATO SAUCE
	SALT AND PEPPER, TO TASTE
1/4	TEASPOON ALEPPO PEPPER, OR MORE TO TASTE
1/4	CUP OLIVE OIL
1/4	CUP PARSLEY, CHOPPED
1/4	CUP FRESH MINT, CHOPPED

Cut the zucchini into thick rounds and coarsely chop the tomatoes. Set aside.

In a large skillet, sauté the onions and potatoes until translucent and partly cooked. Add the garlic and the tomato sauce and simmer for a few minutes.

Add the squash, tomatoes and seasonings, except for the mint. Cover and simmer, until cooked through.

Sprinkle with chopped mint before serving. Serve as a side dish or over rice as a vegetarian entrée. Cook's

Notes: This dish works with many of your favorite vegetables.

Stewed Squash

I remember Sitto prepared this spinach dish often during Lent. With its fragrant seasonings, it's such a unique and satisfying vegetarian dish for those of us who would sometimes prefer a meatless meal.

SPINACH AND BLACK-EYED PEAS
SBANIKH W' LUBIYA

1	CUP DRIED BLACK-EYED PEAS
4	CUPS WATER (DIVIDED USE)
7	CLOVES GARLIC, PEELED
2	TEASPOONS WHOLE CORIANDER
1	TABLESPOON SALT
3	YELLOW ONIONS, SLICED THIN
1/2	CUP OLIVE OIL
2	LBS. FRESH SPINACH, WASHED
1/2	TEASPOON PEPPER
	DASH ALEPPO PEPPER
1/2	LEMON

Spinach and Black-Eyed Peas

sort the black-eyed peas in a small bowl. Remove any broken ones or any debris. Rinse the peas and drain.

Boil 2 cups of water in a 3 qt. pan. Remove from the heat and add the peas to soak, covered, for 3 hours.

Drain the peas after soaking, add 2 more cups of cold water. Bring to a boil and then lower to a simmer, covered, for about 45 minutes to an hour or until cooked. When cooked, drain the peas, cover and set aside.

While the peas cook, crush the garlic cloves, coriander and salt in a mortar and pestle, or use a blender or food processor. (See Cook's Notes.)

In a 12" skillet, fry the onions in the oil until browned, being careful not to burn them. When they are browned, add the garlic/spice/salt mixture to the onions and stir to sauté a minute or two. Add the peas, stir and then remove from the heat and keep covered.

In a 3 qt. saucepan, cook the spinach in 1" of water for just a few minutes and drain well.

Add the spinach to the skillet of onions and black-eyed peas and toss. Simmer for a few minutes to blend the flavors. Add fresh ground black pepper, Aleppo Pepper and squeeze the half lemon over all and toss. Check for seasoning and adjust, adding more salt or pepper if needed. Let the spinach stand, covered, for a few minutes before serving.

Cook's Notes: For added flavor, I sometimes heat the coriander in a dry frying pan to release the oils before grinding them in my spice grinder.

I have substituted a can of drained black-eyed peas when I'm rushed.

As with most dishes, Sitto would not use much meat, allowing the vegetables to be the focal point of a meal and in keeping with Syrian cuisine. Meat was almost a token to her, more to prove we could still afford it on the table than that we needed it.

CAULIFLOWER WITH MEAT
ZAHRA MA' LAHMEH

1	**MEDIUM YELLOW ONION**
1	**HEAD CAULIFLOWER**
1/2	**LB. GROUND LAMB (COARSELY GROUND) OR GROUND BEEF**
1 1/2	**TEASPOONS SALT (DIVIDED USE)**
	PEPPER TO TASTE
1	**TEASPOON GROUND ALLSPICE**
1/4	**CUP OLIVE OIL**
1	**CLOVE GARLIC, MINCED**
1	**15 OZ. CAN DICED OR CHOPPED TOMATOES**

Cauliflower with Meat

Chop the onion and set aside.

Break the cauliflower into small flowerets and soak in a 3 qt. bowl in 1/2 teaspoon of salted water while preparing the meat.

Mix the meat with the remaining salt, pepper and allspice in a 2 qt. bowl to blend.

In a deep 5 qt. pan or Dutch oven, sauté the meat and onion in the olive oil until the onions and meat are lightly browned. Add the minced garlic at the end and toss lightly through. Do not brown the garlic. Drain the tomatoes, reserving the juice. Add the tomatoes to the meat and lower to a simmer.

Rinse the cauliflower in cold water, drain and then add to the meat mixture. Mix and continue to simmer, covered, for 30 to 45 minutes or until the cauliflower is cooked. While simmering, add the reserved tomato juice, if needed.

We didn't have fried foods very often, so this was a real treat when Sitto served it. In her day, she chose these vegetables when they were in season and plentiful. Today, we are fortunate to have these vegetables whenever we want them. This is a great side dish or if it's a meatless meal, why not just serve these crunchy vegetables with soup or salad and warm Syrian bread!

FRIED CAULIFLOWER AND ZUCCHINI
ZAHRA W'KUSA MITLI

1	HEAD CAULIFLOWER
2	ZUCCHINI SQUASH
1	CUP OIL, OR MORE IF NEEDED
2	BEATEN EGGS
	SALT AND PEPPER, TO TASTE
2	CUPS PLAIN OR FLAVORED BREAD CRUMBS, OR MORE IF NEEDED

Break the cauliflower into flowerets and soak in a 5 qt. pot with cold, salted water for a few minutes. Rinse and drain.

Add fresh water to cover and blanch the cauliflower in boiling water for 2 to 3 minutes, until only partially cooked. Drain and cool on paper towels.

Dip the cauliflowerets into the beaten egg and then the bread crumbs. Set aside.

Heat the oil in a 12" skillet or deep fryer. Drop the flowerets into the oil and fry until golden. Drain on paper towels and immediately season with salt and pepper.

To prepare fresh zucchini: Place the squash, quartered or sliced, into a colander and salt overall. Allow to drain for 15 minutes. Blot with paper toweling and then fry in oil, with or without the above egg wash and bread crumbs. Immediately season with salt and pepper.

Cook's Notes: Sitto would sometimes prepare the cauliflower without egg or bread crumbs. If so, be sure to dry the cauliflower completely before frying.

RICE, GRAINS, LEGUMES, PASTA

My younger sister Elaine was still at home and close to our grandmother in those later years after I married. Elaine fondly remembers this dish as the Syrian "Rice-a-Roni." It was a typical accompaniment to many meals that our Sitto made. I'm so glad she got the recipe!

RICE WITH NOODLES
RIZ B' SHA'RIYA

1/2	CUP FINE NOODLES, VERMICELLI OR CUT FIDEO NOODLES
3	CUPS BROTH OR WATER
1	CUP RICE, RAW, RINSED AND DRAINED
1	TEASPOON SALT, TO TASTE (USE LESS IF USING CANNED BROTH)
2	TABLESPOONS CLARIFIED BUTTER OR MARGARINE
1/4	CUP OLIVE OIL
1	YELLOW ONION, THINLY SLICED

Rice With Noodles

Break the noodles into 1" pieces. Place in a shallow baking pan and toast under a broiler, turning frequently, for a few minutes until browned.

Fill a 5 qt. pan with the broth or water, rice, salt and butter. Bring to a boil, add the noodles, stir and cover. Lower the heat to a simmer until the liquid is absorbed and the rice is cooked. Check to make sure you don't need more water before the rice is finished cooking. The rice will finish with holes all over the top of it in approximately 20 minutes.

While the rice cooks, heat the olive oil in a 10" skillet. Add the onions and sauté until browned and caramelized. Keep the heat moderate to prevent the onions from burning.

Pour the caramelized onions and oil over the rice and noodle mixture and mix them in before serving.

Our whole family loved Sitto's Syrian stuffing. She would usually serve it as a side dish to lamb or poultry dishes. Considering the protein content, this makes a substantial main dish, if you'd like.

SITTO NAIMA'S SYRIAN STUFFING
HASHWEH'T SITTO NAIMA

2	**CUPS RICE, RAW, RINSED**
4	**CUPS WATER**
1 1/2	**TEASPOONS SALT (DIVIDED USE)**
1	**15 OZ. CAN CHICKPEAS (GARBANZO BEANS) DRAINED, RINSED**
3/4	**LB. GROUND LAMB (COARSE GRIND)**
1	**TEASPOON GROUND ALLSPICE**
1/2	**TEASPOON DATAH SPICE (SEE GLOSSARY)**
1	**TABLESPOON OLIVE OIL**

Sitto Naima's Syrian Stuffing

Place the rice, water, 1/2 teaspoon salt and drained chickpeas in a large 5 qt. pot. Bring to a boil and then lower to a simmer, cover and cook for 20 minutes or until the rice is tender.

In a 3 qt. bowl, mix the ground lamb, allspice, Datah spice and teaspoon of salt.

In a 12" skillet, heat the oil and then sauté the seasoned lamb until browned. When the meat is cooked, add it to the cooked rice and chickpeas. Toss together and serve.

Cook's Notes: An option to the chickpeas would be 1/2 cup of pine nuts. Add them to the lamb mixture as it sautés and just before stirring into the rice.

The first time I saw the Narghile, now known as the Hooka, I was amazed. My grandmother's cousin sat cross-legged on the carpet, with a serene look on his face, puffing away at his bubbling water pipe. His intriguing pipe, filled with a sweet-smelling tobacco, looked so unusual to a child. I always thought it looked like fun and wondered why the ladies never tried it!

RICE PILAF
RIZ B' SANOBAR

6	TABLESPOONS CLARIFIED BUTTER (DIVIDED USE) OR MARGARINE
1/2	CUP ONIONS, DICED
1/2	CUP CARROTS, DICED
4	CUPS WATER OR STOCK
1/2	TEASPOON GROUND ALLSPICE
1	TEASPOON DATAH SPICE (SEE GLOSSARY)
	DASH TUMERIC
1/2	TEASPOON SALT, OR TO TASTE
	DASH PEPPER
2	CUPS RICE, RAW, RINSED AND DRAINED
1/4	CUP PINE NUTS

In a large 5 qt. pot, heat 4 tablespoons of the butter to sauté the onions and the carrots until tender and the onions are translucent.

Pour the water or stock into the onions and carrots. Add the spices, salt and pepper and bring to a boil. Add the rice, stir and cover. Lower the heat to a simmer for 20 minutes or until the liquid is absorbed and the rice is cooked. Keep covered and set aside.

In an 8" skillet, sauté the pine nuts in 2 tablespoons of the butter until golden. Pour the butter and nuts over the rice and cover the pan for 5 minutes.

Toss together and serve.

Cook's Notes: Use vegetable or chicken stock, if preferred.

The pilaf can be updated with 1/4 cup of golden raisins or chopped dried apricots for color and sweetness, if preferred.

Through the years, I had been trying to duplicate my Sitto Naima's perfect rice and lentil pilaf, which she made so often. Long ago, she gave me sketchy instructions, such as rice and lentils, salt and water, as is so typical of Arab cooks. Ratios were always given from mother to daughter as they cooked together and the details would be in memory. Cooking always brings the memory of my grandmother back to me as I marvel at how effortless her creations seemed at the time and sometimes, how difficult to emulate.

RICE AND LENTIL PILAF
MUJEDT'IL RIZ

3/4	CUP LARGE BROWN LENTILS – REMOVE ANY STONES, RINSE & DRAIN
4	CUPS WATER
1/2	CUP OLIVE OIL
2	LARGE YELLOW ONIONS, SLICED THIN
1	CUP LONG GRAIN WHITE RICE, RINSED AND DRAINED
1 1/4	TEASPOONS SALT, OR TO TASTE

Rice and Lentil Pilaf

In a 5 qt. pot, bring the lentils to a boil in the 4 cups of water and simmer covered for approximately 20 minutes until tender.

While the lentils cook, sauté the onions in the heated olive oil in a large 12" skillet. Brown them over moderate heat to caramelize to a dark brown, being careful not to burn them. Remove 1/2 cup of the onions and reserve them for a garnish. Set aside both onion portions, including any oil that remains on them or in the pan.

Drain the lentils, reserving the liquid in a measuring cup and adding any water needed to make 2 3/4 cups. Return the lentils, rice and the liquid to the pot. Add the salt and the larger portion of the caramelized onions. Stir, then cover and simmer for 20 minutes.

When the rice and lentils are cooked and all the liquid is absorbed, place on a platter, adding the 1/2 cup of onion garnish to the top. Serve at once.

Cook's Notes: Lentils do not need to be soaked before cooking. The cooking time varies and may need to be increased with older lentils. Sitto used the large brown lentils, now available at on-line Middle Eastern markets. I have used the smaller brown ones and they are fine.

Bulgar Wheat, a real staple on Sitto's weekly menu, was another healthy family favorite. And now I know why she stayed so young looking. It was full of vitamin E!

BULGAR WHEAT WITH CHICKPEAS AND ONIONS
BURGHUL MA' HUMMUS

4	YELLOW ONIONS, MEDIUM (DIVIDED USE)
3	CUPS STOCK OR WATER
1 1/2	TEASPOONS SALT, OR TO TASTE
2	CUPS BULGAR WHEAT (#3 COARSE GRAIN)
1	15 OZ. CAN CHICKPEAS (GARBANZO BEANS) DRAINED, RINSED
4	TABLESPOONS OLIVE OIL

Cut three of the onions in quarters.

In a 5 qt. pot, boil the onion quarters in 3 cups of the stock or salted water. Simmer until the onions are partly cooked.

In a 2 qt. bowl, wash and rinse the Bulgar once in cold water. Drain and add to the onions along with the chickpeas. Bring to a boil and then lower to simmer, cover and cook approximately 15 to 20 minutes. Check to make sure the water is not all absorbed before the wheat is cooked. If needed, add more water. After 15 minutes, check the Bulgar to make sure it is tender but still chewy and that the seasoning is sufficient.

While the Bulgar cooks, slice the fourth onion vertically into thin slices.

In a 10" skillet, fry the onion in the oil to caramelize it. Use moderate heat in order to avoid burning them. Add the browned onion and oil to the cooked Bulgar. Cover and let stand for 15 minutes before tossing and serving.

Cook's Notes: If using vegetable stock or chicken stock, it may be necessary to lessen the salt in the recipe.

It should be noted that Bulgar wheat comes in three sizes of grains. #1 and #2 are used in meat dishes and #3 is a coarser grain and used alone.

I always use a diffuser on the burner for rice and grains to make sure they do not burn or dry out. The chickpeas can be eliminated for a simpler Bulgar wheat dish.

Bulgar Wheat With Chickpeas and Onions

One day, Sitto reminisced about her early life as a young girl in Aleppo. One of the more difficult and frustrating traditions for a young Syrian girl was that her brothers insisted that she be accompanied by one of them whenever they were out. Even after arriving here in America, the old ways were still intact, as her older brothers didn't even want her going out onto the porch alone! As I think back, this same woman later made her new life here, working after her husband died, taking buses to her job and being very much "the modern woman." What a change she saw in her lifetime!

BULGAR WHEAT AND LENTILS
MUJEDARRA

2	YELLOW ONIONS, MEDIUM SIZE
3/4	CUP BROWN LENTILS
1	CUP BULGAR WHEAT, COARSE GRIND #3
3 1/2	CUPS WATER OR STOCK
1 1/2	TEASPOONS SALT
1/4	CUP OLIVE OIL

Cut the onions vertically into thin slices. Set aside.

In a small bowl, clean and sort the lentils, removing any stones. Rinse and drain.

In a measuring cup or bowl, wash and rinse the Bulgar, once, in cold water and drain.

In a 5 qt. Dutch oven or pot, heat the water or stock and bring to a boil. Then add the lentils with the salt and cover. Simmer until the lentils are cooked, about 15 to 20 minutes.

Add the Bulgar wheat to the lentils, cover and simmer for 15 to 20 more minutes, over low heat. At about 15 minutes, check the Bulgar to make sure the water is not all absorbed. If needed, add more water and check to see if the seasoning is sufficient.

While the Bulgar and lentils cook, brown the onions in oil in a 12" skillet until caramelized. Remove from the heat and set aside.

When the Bulgar is cooked, it will be tender but still chewy. Remove from the heat and keep covered for 5 minutes.

Reserving about 1/4 cup of the onions for the garnish, pour the rest, along with the oil into the Bulgar. Mix and serve on a platter with the rest of the caramelized onions as garnish.

Cook's Notes: Vegetable or chicken stock may be substituted for the water. If using stock, lessen the salt in the recipe. In this case, use 1/2 the salt and only add more if needed.

BULGAR WHEAT AND LAMB PILAF
BURGHUL MA' LAHMEH

1	**CUP BULGAR WHEAT, COARSE GRIND #3**
3/4	**LB. GROUND LAMB (COARSE GRIND)**
1	**TEASPOON GROUND ALLSPICE**
1/2	**TEASPOON DATAH SPICE (SEE GLOSSARY)**
1 1/2	**TEASPOONS SALT (DIVIDED USE)**
1	**TABLESPOON OLIVE OIL**
1	**MEDIUM YELLOW ONION, CHOPPED**
3	**CUPS WATER OR STOCK**
1	**8 OZ. CAN TOMATO SAUCE**

In a small bowl, rinse the Bulgar wheat in cold water. Drain and set aside.

In a 3 qt. bowl, mix the ground lamb, allspice, Datah spice and 1 teaspoon of salt.

In a 5 qt. pot, heat the oil. Add the onion and the seasoned lamb. Sauté them until the onion is translucent and the meat is browned.

Add the 3 cups water or broth, Bulgar, 1/2 teaspoon salt and tomato sauce to the meat/onion mixture. Stir and bring the water to a boil. Cover and lower to a simmer for 15 to 20 minutes.

At a mid point, check to make sure that all the liquid has not been absorbed before the wheat is cooked. If necessary, add more water. When the wheat is cooked, it will be tender but still chewy. Remove from the heat and set aside, covered, for 5 minutes. Toss and serve on a platter.

Cook's Notes: Grains always taste richer in a vegetable or chicken stock, if available. The salt content may be reduced if using stock.

Ground beef may substituted for the lamb, if preferred.

Bulgar Wheat and Lamb Pilaf

This pasta dish is real peasant fare that I remember Sitto served as the main entree on a Lenten Friday. My own children loved it years later. When they were younger, one favored the pasta and the other the beans. And my son took out all the onions! Either way, it was a staple in my youth and theirs.

PASTA AND CHICKPEAS
MUGRABIYA

6	SMALL YELLOW OR WHITE ONIONS, PEELED
4	CUPS WATER
1 1/2	TEASPOONS SALT
4	TABLESPOONS CLARIFIED BUTTER OR MARGARINE
1	CUP ACINI DE PEPE PASTA (TINY DOT PASTA)
1	14 OZ. CAN CHICKPEAS (GARBANZO BEANS), RINSED AND DRAINED

Pasta and Chickpeas

Place the peeled onions into a 3 qt. pot. Add the water and salt. Bring to boil, cover and simmer for about 10 minutes or until the onions are tender but still whole.

In the meantime, melt the butter in a 10" skillet. Add the pasta and stir frequently to lightly toast. Remove from the heat.

Gradually add the pasta to the simmering onions, carefully, so as not to splash back. Cover and continue simmering, stirring often, for about 15 minutes.

Add the chickpeas and continue cooking, uncovered, until all the water is absorbed and the pasta is tender and cooked. This may take up to 10 minutes or more.

ORZO AND SPINACH
MACAROONEH MA' SBANIKH

1	**CLOVE GARLIC**
1/2	**TEASPOON CORIANDER SEEDS**
	DASH SALT
1/2	**CUP CHOPPED YELLOW ONION**
1/4	**CUP CLARIFIED BUTTER OR MARGARINE**
1	**CUP ORZO PASTA**
1 1/2	**CUPS WATER OR VEGETABLE STOCK**
4	**CUPS FRESH BABY SPINACH LEAVES, WASHED, STEMS REMOVED**

Orzo and Spinach

Mash the garlic, coriander and dash of salt in a mortar and pestle. Use a blender or food processor, if preferred.

In a 5 qt. pot, lightly sauté the onions in the butter until translucent. Add the pasta and sauté until golden. Then add the crushed garlic and seasonings and stir for a few seconds.

Pour the stock into the pasta, onions and seasonings, bring to a boil, stir, cover and lower the heat to a simmer. The pasta will cook in about 8 to 10 minutes.

Remove the lid, add the spinach leaves, stirring for 2 to 3 minutes until the spinach is wilted and just cooked. Serve as a vegetarian or side dish to an entrée.

Cook's Notes: Chicken stock may be substituted for the vegetable stock, if preferred.

Barley Pilaf

This fragrant pilaf is almost a meal in itself! It's a really good vegetarian dish on its own or as a nice accompaniment to grilled lamb or chicken.

BARLEY PILAF
SHA'IR

1	CUP BARLEY, HULLED (NOT PEARL), RINSED AND DRAINED
3 1/2	CUPS WATER
1	CINNAMON STICK
1/4	CUP GOLDEN RAISINS
1/4	CUP DARK RAISINS
1/4	CUP CHOPPED DRIED APRICOTS (OPTIONAL)
1/4	CUP CHOPPED PITTED DATES
1 1/2	TEASPOONS GROUND FENNEL SEEDS
1 1/2	TEASPOONS GROUND ANISE SEED
1/2	TEASPOON GROUND CINNAMON
1/2	CUP SLIVERED ALMONDS
4	TABLESPOONS BUTTER (DIVIDED USE)
1/8	CUP CHOPPED, UNSALTED PISTACHIO NUTS (OPTIONAL TOPPING)

Place the water and barley in a large 5 qt. pot and bring to a boil. Lower the heat to a simmer and add the cinnamon stick and stir once. (Stirring often causes the barley to become creamy and sticky.) Cover and cook without stirring for about 45 minutes or until the grains are tender but chewy. After 40 minutes, check the tenderness of the barley and also make sure that the water has not evaporated. Add more water, if needed.

In the last 5 minutes of cooking, add the raisins, apricots and dates. Continue to simmer until the barley is tender but slightly chewy and the fruit has softened. Turn off the heat and keep covered.

Combine the ground spices in a cup and mix well to blend. Set aside.

Lightly toast the slivered almonds in 2 tablespoons of the butter over low heat in an 8" skillet. Turn off the heat and add the rest of the butter to melt.

If necessary, drain any excess liquid remaining in the barley mixture. Add the ground spices to the barley and mix. Then pour the butter and almonds onto the barley and toss to blend. Cover the pot again and let stand for 5 minutes.

To serve: Place the pilaf on a platter. Top with the chopped pistachio nuts for color and added texture, if desired.

Cook's Notes: I have also substituted toasted pine nuts or walnuts in place of the almonds.

Use fresh spices ground in a spice grinder for the best flavor. Spices can be increased or decreased, depending on your taste.

PASTRIES, SWEETS, NUTS

Those Incredible Butter Cookies

My favorite story regarding this simple and scrumptious cookie recipe points out that while we can slavishly follow a recipe, sometimes things just won't go right.

My mother-in-law Mary's recipe was very precise. She had been making this delicacy for years to rave reviews. One day, while in the middle of making these cookies, she got into a "Lucy Riccardo" type of situation. As she told it, when everything was measured and mixed, the dough refused to hold together in order to form these "bracelet-like" cookies. She sent my father-in-law to the store for more flour. The dough still wouldn't work together enough to roll the cookies. She then sent him for more sugar because now there was too much flour to the sugar ratio. Then she needed more butter, etc. etc. You guessed it. After 10 lbs. of dough, which was enough to feed an army, she still couldn't get the dough to work together!

I have since discovered that the climate, temperature of the dough and possibly mystical influences can give you a harder time of it with this incredibly simple recipe. See my cook's notes for tips on avoiding all this hassle. I promise that once you have made these cookies, you'll be "famous" for them!

THOSE INCREDIBLE BUTTER COOKIES FROM MARY JWEID
GHRAYBEH'T MARY JWEID

4	CUPS CLARIFIED BUTTER, WARM, BASICS, PAGE 7
4	CUPS SUGAR
8	CUPS FLOUR

In a stand mixer set on medium speed, mix the warmed butter and sugar until very well blended. Add the flour gradually to form a dough. Let the dough rest for 15 minutes.

The dough will start to hold together and can be pinched into shape with your fingers. See Cook's Notes.

On a very lightly floured board, roll about 2 tablespoons of dough into a finger-shaped roll, to form a bracelet. This should be about 2 1/2" in diameter.

Preheat the oven to 400 degrees.

Place the cookies on an ungreased baking sheet and bake for 7 to 8 minutes. The cookies will be white, but with a light golden bottom. The tops will appear somewhat dry or with "pores." This will indicate they are perfectly baked. Cool completely before removing them from the cookie sheets, as they will break.

Plastic storage containers with sheets of waxed paper between the layers of cookies will keep them from breaking and prevent freezer burn. Cover the container tightly to store or freeze. This recipe makes abut 60 cookies.

Cook's Notes: If you find the dough will not hold together, try chilling the dough. However, when you first take out the chilled dough, it may be easier to wait a few minutes before beginning to shape them. If it doesn't work for you, gradually add up to an additional 1/2 cup of flour at this time, if necessary. Proceed with rolling out shapes.

If unsure about the consistency when first making these cookies, as I was years ago, I would suggest baking one or two to make sure they do not flatten in the oven. This would indicate that the dough would need more flour. However, proceed with caution, as too much flour will toughen the cookie.

This recipe's ratio can be used to make more or less of these cookies, but remember, the butter and sugar are always equal, with the flour being double that amount.

Only use clarified butter, not sweet butter or margarine.

For ease in blending, use Baker's Sugar. Mix very warm butter and sugar for about 10 minutes to make sure it's blended.

Use an ice cream scoop to use as a gauge for a similar amount of dough each time before rolling.

Chill the dough between batches to keep it cool.

Sitto Naima's Butter Cookies (Unbaked)

My earliest memory of my grandmother's parlor was its very formal look. It was usually closed off until guests came and then Sitto would welcome her guests with "Ahlan Wa Sahlan," a wish for God's blessing given to all who visit. Wonderful sweets like Ghraybeh would be a typical offering.

SITTO NAIMA'S BUTTER COOKIES
GHRAYBEH'T SITTO NAIMA

4	CUPS CLARIFIED BUTTER, WARM, BASICS, PAGE 7
4	CUPS SUGAR
1/2	CUP SEMOLINA (SMEDE)
8	CUPS FLOUR
	BLANCHED ALMONDS (OPTIONAL)

Mix the warm butter and sugar in a mixer until well blended.

In a 5 qt. bowl or pot, mix the semolina and flour with your hands to blend and then add the butter/sugar mixture. Knead just until the mixture sticks together and forms into firmer dough.

Roll into a thin cigar shape about 6" long and then attach the ends to form a bracelet. Add an almond half to seal the ends. Traditionally, a sliced almond half is placed on this joint.

Preheat the oven to 400 degrees.

Place the cookies on ungreased baking sheets and bake for 7 to 8 minutes. The tops will be white and appear to look dry with textured "pores." The bottom should be no more than light gold. Cool on the baking sheet before removing. Store in a tightly covered container.

Cooks Notes: This recipe differs from my mother-in-law's due to the addition of semolina. Therefore, it's not necessary to add more flour. If you find that the dough is not coming together to form the cookies, set aside for about 15 to 20 minutes and you'll find the consistency has changed and is more workable. The reason for this is that the butter will have cooled.

To blanch almonds: Cover the shelled nuts with boiling water and let steep for about 3 to 5 minutes. Rinse with cold water, drain and remove the skins. Dry and use immediately or store in a covered container.

The almonds are optional. As a girl, I remember taking the almond off before eating the cookie! This recipe may be successfully cut in half.

Sitto Naima's Butter Cookies, Baked

Memories of my grandmother, sitting at her kitchen table shelling walnuts, often comes to mind as I reach for the nuts needed in a recipe. We would sit and talk sometimes as she opened each one and carefully removed the halves. I usually managed to pop a few walnuts into my mouth to savor. They were a great treat that was always available for snacking and baking and an integral part of all Syrian baking.

Whether it's known as Baklava in Greece or Butlawa in Syria, this universal sweet is much loved by us all. Although the Greek version uses honey, the Syrian cooks used our basic Simple Sugar Syrup called Shirreh, made with Orange Blossom Water or, as some preferred, Rose Water. I remember making Butlawa with my mother-in-law and couldn't believe how easy it was to make. Yes, I said easy!

TRADITIONAL BAKLAVA
BUTLAWA

	SUGAR SYRUP (SHIRREH) - BASICS, PAGE 6 - ROOM TEMPERATURE - TO TASTE
1 1/2	LBS. BUTTER, CLARIFIED - BASICS, PAGE 7
1 1/2	LBS. SHELLED WALNUTS, CHOPPED FINE
5	TABLESPOONS SUGAR, OR MORE TO TASTE
1	TABLESPOON ORANGE BLOSSOM WATER (MAHZAHAD)
1	LB. PHYLLO PASTRY
1/2	LB. CRISCO SHORTENING
	BASTING BRUSH

Prepare the sugar syrup (Shirreh) the day before or early in the day, according to the recipe on page 6.

Clarify the 1 1/2 lbs. of butter according to the basic recipe on page 7. Keep both at room temperature.

In a 1 qt. bowl, add the sugar to the walnuts and then the Orange Blossom Water, mix and set aside.

Melt the Crisco and the clarified butter together in a medium saucepan or the microwave and set aside.

In a large 9" x 12" rectangular or round 15" x 2-1/2" metal baking pan: Pour some of the melted butter mixture to cover the bottom.

Layer 3 whole sheets of phyllo, allowing the paper to overlap the pan. This will keep the walnuts inside the phyllo when serving the end pieces. If your pan is round, alternate the sheets around to overlap it. After 3 or 4 layers, baste the butter mixture to the top sheet. Continue layering to the mid point of the pan.

After filling half of the phyllo into the pan, layer the walnut mixture evenly over all. Continue with the rest of the layered phyllo, basting the butter more generously, between every third sheet. When finished layering, baste more butter over the top, reserving 1/4 to 1/2 cup. Cover and cool in the refrigerator for about an hour.

Preheat the oven to 350 degrees.

Remove the pan from the refrigerator and using a sharp knife, make diagonal cuts every 2 inches across the pan. Then reverse the direction and repeat the 2" diagonal cuts to form diamond shapes.

Baste the top with the rest of the reserved butter. Cover with parchment paper, extending to the outside of the pan and bake on the middle rack of the oven for 1/2 hour. Then move the pan from the middle rack to the upper rack and bake for another 1/2 hour.

Towards the end of baking, check under the parchment. If the phyllo layers seem to be separating, remove the paper and allow the top to brown for about 5 more minutes. When the top is lightly browned, remove from the oven and drain any excess butter. Immediately pour room temperature sugar syrup over all. Cool completely. Before serving, slice the diamond shapes again into the previous cuts. Keep in a cool place but not refrigerated.

Cook's Notes: At the time we baked together, my mother-in-law used brown paper to top the Butlawa during baking, which is still an alternative to parchment paper. The idea is to keep the top layers of phyllo from browning too soon before the rest of the layers have baked. Do not use foil.

Phyllo can be purchased in one pound boxes in the freezer case of most supermarkets and in Middle Eastern stores.

Frozen phyllo should be defrosted slowly in its package in the refrigerator for 8 hours or the day before using. A fast thaw will cause condensation in the pastry package. Do not refreeze after defrosting. Unfrozen phyllo should only be left in original packaging at room temperature for up to 4 hours before baking with it.

When handling, keep the opened phyllo covered with plastic wrap or wax paper and then covered with a damp towel to keep the paper-thin sheets from drying out. Open and take out only those sheets you will be immediately working with, keeping the rest wrapped and refrigerated. Any direct draft will also dry out the sheets.

Traditional Baklava

Although the literal translation in Arabic is "fingers," as kids we always called them "cigars". They were easy to eat and as I later found out, easy to make. If you haven't worked with Phyllo dough sheets before, why not try these delectable rolled "fingers" filled with walnuts. And if you have baked with it, this recipe makes good use of any leftover Phyllo. It is very similar in taste to Baklava and wonderful with Arab Coffee, Qahwa.

SWEET PHYLLO FINGERS
ASABIH HILU

1	LB. CLARIFIED BUTTER, BASICS, PAGE 7
1	LB. SHELLED WALNUTS, CHOPPED FINE
1/2	CUP SUGAR
1	TEASPOON ORANGE BLOSSOM WATER (MAHZAHAD)
1/2	LB. PHYLLO PASTRY
2	CUPS SUGAR SYRUP (SHIRREH), BASICS, PAGE 6 - ROOM TEMPERATURE

Clarify the butter according to the Basics Recipe. Set aside or refrigerate until needed. Warm before preparing the pastries.

Prepare the nut mixture by mixing the walnuts, sugar and Orange Blossom Water in a small bowl and set aside.

Cut the phyllo sheets in half lengthwise. Take 2 sheets and brush the top sheet with butter. Spoon 3 tablespoons of the walnut mixture evenly down the vertical length of the pastry. Roll the sheets into a long cigar shape and brush with more butter.

Sweet Phyllo Fingers

Preheat the oven to 350 degrees.

Place the rolled pastry onto a greased or parchment covered baking sheet. Repeat and make more cigar lengths with the rest of the phyllo and nut filling.

Bake for 20 minutes until golden brown. Remove from the oven and drizzle room temperature sugar syrup over the pastry. Set aside.

Cool completely, for about an hour, then cut into shorter "finger" lengths and serve.

Cook's Notes: See the Baklava recipe for tips on working with phyllo.

Traditionally, the women of Syria and Lebanon wore several gold bracelets on their wrists. They were typically hand-carved with diamond-cut embossing all around the gleaming gold. My grandmother's friends never removed them, busily working in their kitchens with these tinkling Middle Eastern bangle bracelets.

In the late 1950's, my mother's good friend, Katherine Ged, went back to Syria, Lebanon and Egypt for a visit. Upon her return, my mother surprised me with the gold bracelets she had purchased for me from her friend. The yellow gold bangles, with a beautiful hand-cut floral design worked all around them, shone like diamonds on my slender wrist. It was a glint of my grandmother's homeland and I felt like a princess.

LADY'S BRACELETS
SUWARI IL' SITT

1 1/2	LBS. CLARIFIED BUTTER, BASICS, PAGE 7
1	LB. SHELLED WALNUTS, FINELY CHOPPED
3	TABLESPOONS SUGAR
1	TEASPOON ORANGE BLOSSOM WATER (MAHZAHAD)
1	LB. PHYLLO PASTRY
1	DOWEL, 1/4" DIAMETER X 18" LONG (SEE COOK'S NOTES)
1	CUP SUGAR SYRUP (SHIRREH) BASICS, PAGE 6 - ROOM TEMPERATURE

Prepare the clarified butter according to the recipe in Basics.

In a 3 qt. bowl, mix the walnuts, sugar and Orange Blossom Water and set aside.

Preheat the oven to 350 degrees.

Generously grease the bottom of a lipped baking sheet with some clarified butter.

Place a sheet of phyllo on a work surface. Then take the dowel and roll it against the phyllo, winding the phyllo around the dowel. Then squeeze the sheet of phyllo together towards the middle of the dowel as you gather or shirr the phyllo paper.

Then slide the phyllo off the dowel. Crimp the phyllo onto a circle, pressing and overlapping the bottom dough into a flat base to hold the nut filling. As you work, place each "bracelet" into a muffin tin to help hold them together before filling. Then fill the round circles of phyllo with the chopped walnut mixture.

Place each bracelet on the baking sheet, drizzle each with butter and bake for 15 minutes until lightly golden. Remove from the oven and immediately drizzle the room temperature sugar syrup over the hot pastry.

Cook's Notes: A thin wooden dowel or rod, or even a long-handled wooden spoon will help to shape the phyllo bracelets. The dowel is used as a tool to gather the dough tightly. Once gathered, the ends of the phyllo become a platform on which to place the nut filling.

My sister Elaine recalls her trip to Greece as even more memorable when she noted the aroma of Mahlab wafting on the wind. It reminded her of our Sitto's pastries, like Karrabij.

These wonderful filled egg-shaped sweets were always made at Easter time, as the egg is symbolic for this most holy of Christian holidays. The cookie is filled with a walnut mixture and then baked and topped with a unique frosting called Nataef. This shiny white fondant-like frosting is sprinkled with cinnamon for a delectable and famous Aleppo treat for the senses...taste and sight!

ALEPPO STUFFED COOKIES
KARRABIJ HALABY

5 1/4	CUPS CLARIFIED BUTTER OR 3 LBS. TO BE CLARIFIED - BASICS, PAGE 7
10	CUPS SEMOLINA (SMEDE)
3 1/3	CUPS FLOUR
1/2	TEASPOON SALT
3 1/2	TABLESPOONS GROUND BLACK CHERRY KERNELS (MAHLAB) SEE GLOSSARY
3 - 5	CUPS WARM WATER

Prepare the clarified butter according to the Basics Recipe.

Mix the dry ingredients and spice in a large 8 qt.pot until well blended.

Gradually add the room-temperature butter and mix. Then add the warm water until the mixture is completely blended. Knead until the dough is smooth and stiff, about 5 minutes. Set aside, covered, for two hours.

Nut Filling:

6	CUPS SHELLED WALNUTS, FINELY CHOPPED
4	TABLESPOONS SUGAR
3 - 4	TEASPOONS ORANGE BLOSSOM WATER (MAHZAHAD) TO TASTE

In a 2 qt. bowl, blend the nuts, sugar and Orange Blossom Water.

To prepare the cookies:
Make ping-pong sized balls of the dough. With your thumb, make an indentation in the ball. Twirl the dough, using your thumb as a guide and forming it into the shape of an egg. Make sure that the dough thickness is even around the entire egg shape, being careful not to poke a hole in the dough cavity. If you do pierce it, seal it again with your fingers. Make sure the thickness of the inner wall of the egg is consistent.

Preheat the oven to 425 degrees.

Fill the cavity with a heaping teaspoon of the nut mixture. Seal the cookie and shape each end of the dough so that it will look like an egg.

Bake the cookies on an ungreased cookie sheet on the middle rack of the oven for 10 to 15 minutes. The cookie will be light, but with a slight golden color on the bottom. Do not allow the top to brown. Set aside to cool.

Store the cooled cookies at room temperature, tightly covered, until ready to frost with the Nataef recipe to follow.

Cook's Notes: I use a spice grinder to grind the black cherry kernels (Mahlab) to a powder. In my grandmother's day, she would use her mortar and pestle, which was hard work!

I have successfully prepared half of this recipe. As with so many of these old recipes, the women often prepared them with family and in large quantities. This full recipe makes about 120 cookies.

Karrabij and Mahmoul

As a little girl, I watched my grandmother make this mysterious frothy marvel. She would take what looked like pieces of wood, wash them carefully and then boil them in water until the liquid thickened and foamed. I saw her strain this liquid and then beat it until it became frothy. She patiently added her warm sugar syrup, beating it again. Finally, it was all combined with the stiffened egg whites to form a thick, whiter-than-white, shiny and fragrant mass of goodness. It almost had a hint of licorice flavor to it and was definitely an acquired taste for any westerner. Through the years, she made it less and less, I suspect because that mystical ingredient, soapwort root, was harder and harder to obtain. As an adult, I also had the same problem. I marveled over the first person to have tried using the froth from this root to make a sweet delicacy!

While pouring through my cookbooks as a young woman, I began to see that Cream of Tartar accomplished a very similar result. It lacked the unique fragrance and "whiteness" produced by that elusive soapwort root, but the sheen and texture were very close. And it was a lot less like the "bubble and squeak witches brew" of the soapwort!

I remember telling my grandmother that I had tried the cream of tartar. Since it wasn't what she had learned, she was not so convinced. She did, however, proudly tell her friends that I was "experimenting" and had found a substitute.

In further research, I found that the root of the soapwort bush, Saponaria Officinalis, is similar to the South American Quillaja Saponaria tree known as Bois de Panama. Both the bush and the tree produce Saponin, which is the mysterious foaming ingredient. Years ago, I recalled that my mother-in-law referred to the soapwort root as "soapbark" when making the Nataef. Although this is all a great mystery to western cooks, this unusual soapwort plant was growing and readily available in Aleppo, Syria. This may explain why Karrabij and Nataef became a famous and unique specialty of that city.

My grandmother's Nataef recipe, using my cream of tartar as a substitute ingredient, is a close second to her original recipe and far more practical today. I've also included my moth-er-in-law's traditional recipe following this one.

KARRABIJ FROSTING
NATAEF

4	CUPS SUGAR
1 1/2	CUPS WATER
1	TABLESPOON CREAM OF TARTAR
1/2	LEMON OR DASH OF LEMON SALT (SEE GLOSSARY)
4	EGG WHITES
1 - 2	TEASPOONS ORANGE BLOSSOM WATER (MAHZAHAD)
	CINNAMON FOR GARNISH

In a 3 qt. saucepan, bring the sugar and water to a boil and then lower to a simmer. Cover the pan and simmer for about 5 minutes. Then uncover and continue simmering for about 20 to 25 minutes more. Test by dipping a spoon into the sugar syrup, dripping it onto a plate to allow it to cool slightly. The syrup should be thick but able to move when cooled on a plate, not glue-like. Test it often to avoid overcooking, as the syrup needs to be the consistency of thick pancake syrup. Another hint: If it coats the spoon, it may be thick enough.

At the end of the simmer, add the cream of tartar and squeeze the lemon into it (or the dash of lemon salt). Mix and set aside while you whip the egg whites.

In a stand mixer: Whip 4 egg whites on high until frothy and stiff. Then gradually add all of the warm sugar syrup to the egg whites, with the mixer on, until the mixture is "marshmallowy" and shiny. If the syrup has been thickened properly, this should not be as stiff as a divinity cake frosting.

When the mixture has thickened, add the Orange Blossom Water at the end, mixing to blend. Set aside to serve with the Karrabij cookies or refrigerate until serving. The refrigerated frosting (Nataef) will keep for about 2 weeks. If the mixture separates, stir before serving.

To serve Karrabij and Nataef: Place the Karrabij cookies on individual plates and spoon about a tablespoon of the frosting on top of each cookie. Sprinkle with a dash of cinnamon and serve.

For a group serving: Frost the top of each cookie and stack, pyramid style onto a platter. Lightly sprinkle cinnamon over all and serve.

Cook's Notes: Rose Water flavoring is sometimes preferred and may be used in place of the Orange Blossom Water.

I made this recipe with my Mother-in-law, Mary, just once during her visit from the east coast. I do wish I had been more descriptive in my notebook. My notes mention the water amount as 2 to 3 "glasses" rather than measured cups. This was my challenge with her recipes and my grandmother's. The older cooks would use handfuls, pinches and pounds and even favorite glasses as ratios for many dishes. This didn't matter in their day since mothers and their daughters cooked alongside each other daily, passing on these secrets of their ancestors. In my time, I didn't have that luxury and this was the overriding reason for writing this book.

MARY JWEID'S TRADITIONAL NATAEF
NATAEF MIN MARY JWEID

3	OZ. SOAPWORT ROOT, APPROXIMATE (ER El HALAWA) (SEE GLOSSARY)
2	CUPS COLD WATER
2	EGG WHITES
	PREPARED SUGAR SYRUP RECIPE (SHIRREH) BASICS, PAGE 6 - WARM

Pound the soapwort bark into pea-size pieces and wash the bark well through a colander to remove any debris. Soak in a 2 qt. pan with the 2 cups of cold water. Cover and place in the refrigerator for 3 days.

Heat the bark and soaking water in a 2 qt. pan and bring to a boil. As it boils, foam will begin to form at the top of the pan. Watch it carefully, as it will rise. Skim this foam off the top and place it in a bowl and set aside. When the water has been absorbed to about 1/4 of its volume, turn off the heat and pour the pan water through a fine strainer or cheesecloth. Save the water and discard the bark.

Beat the egg whites in an electric mixer, until it forms stiff peaks. Keeping the mixer on, add the foam and then gradually add the bark water. Then begin to add the warm sugar syrup in a stream until the mixture is shiny white and is the consistency of melted marshmallow and somewhat elastic.

Serve at room temperature over Karrabij. The remaining Nataef should be stored in the refrigerator, as needed, for up to 2 weeks. If the mixture separates, mix by hand to blend the syrup back into it before serving.

Cook's Notes: You will require the entire Sugar Syrup recipe for the Nataef.

See the "WHERE TO BUY IT" section of this book for purchasing soapwort. It is also known as soapwort root, soapbark and Bois de Panama. Some sources provide the bark in pieces. It should still be pounded to pea size.

Mahmoul, a traditional filled cookie is an Easter favorite. It's the same cookie recipe as the Karrabij, but larger. The Mahmoul is put into a mold before baking so that it has a wonderful imprint on its top to hold the powdered sugar dusting. This is, by far, a more popular sweet throughout the Middle East. The consistency varies amongst the Arab community from firm to buttery soft. Of course, I prefer my Sitto's Aleppo version.

ALEPPO FILLED COOKIES
MAHMOUL HALABY

Prepare the dough according to the Karrabij recipe, but roll the dough into larger ball portions, about 2 1/2" to 3" for each cookie. Fill each with about 1 heaping tablespoon of the walnut mixture and seal it. Leave the ends rounded and more egg-shaped.

Traditionally, the top of the Mahmoul is decorated by placing it into a hand-carved wooden mold, much like that of a butter mold, but deeper, with a concave egg shape carved inside of it. See the Cook's Notes.

Place the filled dough egg into the mold, pressing lightly with your palm, to imprint it with the pattern. Then turn the filled mold over onto an ungreased baking sheet and tap lightly to release the cookie. This will allow it to bake with the imprint on top.

Mahmoul Molds

Preheat the oven to 425 degrees.
Bake the cookies for 12 to 15 minutes, until light and pale gold on the bottom. Do not allow the top to change color. Set aside to cool. When cooled, sift powdered sugar over the top of the cookie before serving. If not immediately serving, the cookies may be stored, un-sugared, in an airtight container or frozen.
This recipe makes approximately 35 cookies.

Cook's Notes: Mahmoul molds are easily obtainable from Middle Eastern stores. If unavailable, a design may be tweezed on the top of the cookie with blunt-ended tongs or a cookie stamp after the Mahmoul is filled. The top indentations are traditional as they are necessary to hold the powdered sugar.

I remember a wonderful brunch in Brooklyn at my mother's friend Antoinette's table. The memory of those perfect morsels stays with me. I have modernized the memory with a pancake mix, rather than the made-from-scratch version for this traditional Arab sweet. I also wanted to avoid deep-frying these traditional wonders and accommodate more modern tastes. The clarified butter will not burn and adds a rich flavor to the crepes. I've also added the recipe for the alternate nut filling served at the time, which I preferred.

ALEPPO DESSERT CREPES
ATAYEF HALABY

1	16 OZ. CONTAINER RICOTTA CHEESE (WHOLE MILK)
1/4	CUP SUGAR
1	TEASPOON ORANGE BLOSSOM WATER (MAHZAHAD)
2	CUPS PANCAKE MIX
1	CUP MILK OR MORE, IF NEEDED
1	EGG, BEATEN
1/2	LB. CLARIFIED BUTTER, BASICS, PAGE 7
	PREPARED SUGAR SYRUP (SHIRREH) BASICS, PAGE 6 - ROOM TEMPERATURE - TO TASTE

In a 2 qt. bowl, mix the Ricotta cheese and sugar. Add the Orange Blossom Water and mix well. Set

aside. Place a sheet of parchment paper on a baking sheet and set aside.

Mix the milk and egg in a measuring bowl or pitcher. Add the pancake mix and blend, adding more milk, if necessary, to ensure a thin batter.

Heat a non-stick pancake griddle over a medium flame and grease lightly.

Pour about 3 tablespoons of batter onto the griddle. When the top forms holes and the edges appear dry, do not turn over. Remove one pancake at a time onto a plate, with the uncooked side facing up.

Immediately fill the pancake with a tablespoon of the Ricotta mixture. Fold over the pancake and seal the ends firmly with your fingers, to create a turnover with a fluted edge. Place on the parchment paper. And repeat with the rest of the batter.

To prepare for serving:
Melt some of the clarified butter in a large 12" skillet. When the butter is heated, add a few of the pancake crepes at a time, browning them on both sides.

Remove to a platter and immediately drizzle with the prepared sugar syrup. Serve additional syrup for individuals to use, as desired.

Cook's Notes: As an alternate filling, or in addition to the Ricotta, this Walnut Filling is traditionally used. Prepare in advance in this ratio:

1	LB. SHELLED WALNUTS, FINELY CHOPPED
1/4	CUP SUGAR
1	TEASPOON ORANGE BLOSSOM WATER (MAHZAHAD)

In a 2 qt. bowl, mix the walnuts, sugar and Orange Blossom Water.

Fill the pancakes as above using the nut mixture and proceed with the rest of the recipe.

The crepes may be refrigerated or frozen at this point if you are not serving them immediately.

Cook's Notes: If freezing the crepes, freeze them flat on a parchment-covered baking sheet and cover with foil. After they have frozen, they may be placed in plastic containers for future use. When preparing them, defrost for 15 minutes before proceeding with the browning.

These filled crepes are traditionally deep fried and are then dipped into the sugar syrup (Shirreh). I prefer sautéing them in clarified butter and just drizzling the syrup over them, rather than soaking them in syrup, which is the typical and traditional way.

You may want to try them traditionally. If so, fry in a few inches of heated oil in a 10" or 12" skillet to a golden brown. Drain on paper towels and immediately dip into the cold sugar syrup.

Another modern touch would be to eliminate the sugar syrup topping and add any fruit sauce, compote or fresh fruit as a topping. This lighter version also makes a great breakfast or brunch.

Aleppo Dessert Crepes

My grandmother's stovetop rice pudding was another great favorite of mine. Years later, with my own family, Sitto's recipe brought the same enthusiasm. I couldn't keep it in the refrigerator for very long. Although the recipe makes about 8 generous servings, the bowls disappeared faster than I could chill them. The children loved this very creamy pudding and still do!

STOVETOP RICE PUDDING
RIZ B' HALIB

2	QTS. WHOLE MILK (SEE COOK'S NOTES)
2/3	CUP WHITE RICE (UNCOOKED)
3/4	CUPS SUGAR
	CINNAMON FOR GARNISH

Stovetop Rice Pudding

Pour the milk and rice into a 5 qt. pot over medium heat and bring to a boil. Stir the mixture often during this time to prevent the rice from sticking. When the milk starts to boil, lower to a simmer, uncovered, and continue for 45 minutes to 1 hour, stirring occasionally.

Add the sugar and stir. Taste to check for sweetness and if preferred, add more sugar. Continue to simmer for an additional 15 to 20 minutes until the pudding thickens and the rice softens. Stir frequently at this point as the pudding tends to form a skin on top.

When the pudding has thickened, remove from the heat and pour into individual serving bowls or parfait glasses. Sprinkle the tops with cinnamon, cool and then refrigerate before serving.

Cook's Notes: My grandmother would add a cup of water to the milk in order to get the rice to open up without the pudding getting too thick. I have not done so, although, at times, I have added a bit more milk if the rice seems too firm and the pudding is thickening. Remember that the pudding will be thicker when chilled.

I have prepared the pudding with 2% milk and found it works just as well. On the other end of the spectrum, I've added a little evaporated milk at the end and wound up with a very creamy pudding. See what works best for you. I like the rice very cooked and opened up. If firmer rice is preferred, that would mean less cooking time.

I always use a diffuser under my pot to keep the milk from sticking or burning on the bottom. The milk has a tendency to stick to the bottom of the pan if it's not stirred often. Keep a low simmer to avoid turning the pudding into an off-white color.

Icy Pudding

My Mother-in-law, Mary, introduced me to her unique way of serving this traditional Syrian pudding. This refreshing cubed pudding, served with chopped ice and sugar syrup, Shirreh, is one of the most original desserts I've ever eaten. It's a textural and exotic delight that one would find impossible not to slurp! Its origin is as a simple Middle Eastern delicacy, a milk-white cornstarch pudding. This version, however, provides its drama more in the serving than in the preparation. Before air conditioning, it was just the thing to cool off parched and heat-weary guests on a hot August day!

ICY PUDDING
HATALEYA

1	**CUP CORNSTARCH**
1	**CUP COLD WATER**
1	**QT. MILK**
1	**TABLESPOON SUGAR**
2	**CUPS COLD WATER**
	PREPARED SUGAR SYRUP (SHIRREH) BASICS, PAGE 6 - ROOM TEMPERATURE - TO TASTE
	ICE CUBES
	FRESH MINT LEAVES

Set out a 9" x 13" x 2" glass or metal baking pan.

In a measuring cup, mix the cornstarch and cup of cold water until dissolved. Set aside.

In a 3 qt. saucepan, heat the milk over medium heat until just scalded. Add the cornstarch mixture slowly while stirring. Add the sugar and continue to stir. The mixture will begin to thicken.

Cook and stir over low heat for a few more minutes until the mixture is thicker and has an elastic-like consistency when you raise your spoon above the mixture. Then pour all of it into the ungreased pan and allow to cool to room temperature.

When the pudding has cooled, pour the 2 cups of cold water from the measuring cup onto the top of the pudding while holding the back of your hand under the spout. The idea is to avoid piercing the top of the pudding with the water flow. The water will cover the pudding overall by about 1/2".

Cover and chill the pudding for a few hours or overnight.

Place several ice cubes in a baggie and crush coarsely. Return the baggie of ice to the freezer until you're ready to serve.

To serve the pudding:
Set out parfait glasses or glass dessert bowls. Carefully pour out the water from the top of the chilled pudding. Cut the pudding into cubes. It will be the consistency of firm Jell-O.

Pour the prepared room-temperature sugar syrup into a quart pitcher and set aside.

The presentation:
Place a few cubes of pudding into the parfaits. Add some of the crushed ice, drizzle a tablespoon of the sugar syrup, then more pudding cubes and another drizzle of the sugar syrup over all. Use two or three tablespoons of the syrup per dish, or more according to taste and number of servings. Garnish with a mint leaf.

Cook's Notes: The number of pudding cubes per dish will vary based on the size of the serving dish. Keep the pitcher of syrup on hand for additional syrup, if preferred.

The purist will love the texturally exciting taste of the icy pudding and wonderful floral sugar syrup overlay. For some people, this flavoring is an acquired taste. It is possible to substitute Rose Water flavoring in the sugar syrup if you like. The adventurous will love this!

As an alternate: Try the addition of fresh strawberries, blueberries, raspberries or mandarin oranges in addition to the pudding, ice and syrup for an updated taste. Try an edible flower on top for an eye-catching presentation!

Sitto gave me the basic recipe for this Aleppo dessert...but I have to say that I got the refine-ments from my Aunt Mary's mother, Zeheda Farraye. Her style of adding the egg made it much creamier and richer. I have worked with her instructions.

As you can see, the Syrians have made good use of semolina or Smede, as it's known in Arabic, and they prepared it in many unusual ways. Later on, we have successfully used farina in place of the semolina in some of our recipes, like this one, although it is not traditional. Although we westerners think of farina as breakfast food, in our household it was also a rich dessert.

BAKED PUDDING DESSERT, FRENCH STYLE
BUTLAWA FRENGIA

1/4	LB. BUTTER OR MARGARINE (DIVIDED USE)
1	EGG
1/4	CUP COLD MILK
1 1/2	QTS. MILK
3/4	CUP SUGAR
1	CUP FARINA OR SEMOLINA (SMEDE)
1/4	CUP SUGAR FOR TOPPING (FOR GARNISH)
1 1/2	TEASPOONS CINNAMON (FOR GARNISH)

Baked Pudding Dessert, French Style

Prepare a 9" x 13" x 2" rectangular baking pan by greasing it with some of the butter. Reserve the rest of the butter in the refrigerator.

Beat the egg and the 1/4 cup of milk in a measuring cup and set aside.

In a large 5 qt. pot, bring the milk and the 3/4 cup of sugar almost to a boil. Before the milk boils, add the farina, gradually, stirring constantly. Lower to a simmer and cook for about 6 minutes.

Keeping the rest simmering, remove about 1/2 cup of the farina mixture into a small bowl to cool slightly.

Pour the beaten egg/milk mixture into the cooling 1/2 cup of farina and quickly blend. Immediately pour this mixture back into the cooking farina on the stove, stirring briskly and thoroughly to prevent the egg from cooking. Continue to simmer and stir for a few more minutes until the mixture is thick and smooth.

Then pour the cooked farina into the prepared pan and cool at room temperature. Cover the pan with plastic wrap and refrigerate for a few hours or overnight.

Preheat the oven to 450 degrees.

Remove the pudding from the refrigerator and make cuts in the chilled pudding by cutting diagonal rows across the pudding about 2" apart. Then cut crosswise again about 2" apart to form diamond cuts. Each cut piece will be approximately 2" X 2". Do not remove from the pan. Take the remaining butter and slice into teaspoon-sized portions and dot the top of the pudding with them.

Bake for about 40 minutes or until the top is golden brown and the pudding is sizzling.

While the pudding is baking, mix the 1/4 cup of sugar and 1 1/2 teaspoons of cinnamon in a measuring cup for the topping and set aside.

Remove the baked pudding from the oven and immediately sprinkle with the sugar/cinnamon mixture. Allow to cool slightly before serving by slicing again into the diamond shapes. The baked pudding will have a custardy filling with a self-crust top. Serves 8.

Cook's Notes: Use longer-cooking farina, rather than the quick-cook variety if substituting for the semolina. Any leftover pudding should be refrigerated. It may be warmed again in the microwave or oven before serving.

Sitto Naima's Shredded Pastry

This delicious pastry is made throughout Syria and the entire Middle East. I have four versions, the first being the traditional one with a pistachio filling, the next is the one Sitto made more often, possibly because the walnuts were more readily available or less costly. Although Sitto loved the cheese-filled version, she made it less often because some of us found this to be more for an adult palate. Now I think it's scrumptious! The fourth recipe, courtesy of my sister's friend, Arlene, is more westernized but with a traditional filling. All are reminiscent of the best of Syrian sweets and will bring raves.

Sitto Naima's Shredded Pastry, Cut Round

SITTO NAIMA'S SHREDDED PASTRY
KNAIFI'T SITTO NAIMA

1 3/4	**CUPS CLARIFIED OR SWEET BUTTER, MELTED (DIVIDED USE)**
1	**LB. BOX SHREDDED PHYLLO PASTRY (KNAIFI)**
3	**CUPS PISTACHIO NUTS – SHELLED, BLANCHED, FINELY CHOPPED**
4	**TABLESPOONS SUGAR**
2	**TEASPOONS ORANGE BLOSSOM WATER (MAHZAHAD)**
	PREPARED SUGAR SYRUP (SHIRREH) BASICS, PAGE 6 - COLD - TO TASTE

Preheat oven to 350 degrees.

Butter a 9" x 13" x 2" rectangular or oval pan with some of the melted butter. Mix the nuts, sugar and Orange Blossom Water in a small bowl.

In a large 4 qt. bowl, separate the Knaifi dough into pieces. (The pastry is typically long, much like fine pasta.) Separate it into fine strands and then pour the melted butter over all, making sure the pastry strands are well coated.

Pat half of the pastry strands into the bottom of the pan. Add the layer of pistachio nuts and then the remaining half of the pastry. Press down on the pastry layers.

Bake for about 30 to 35 minutes or until golden brown.

Remove from the oven and while still hot, generously pour cold sugar syrup overall. Allow to cool to room temperature before serving by cutting into squares or wedges. Serve warm or at room temperature.

This alternate Walnut Filling may be used instead of the pistachios, if preferred.
Walnut Filling:

3	**CUPS FINELY CHOPPED WALNUTS**
4	**TABLESPOONS SUGAR**
2	**TEASPOONS ORANGE BLOSSOM WATER (MAHZAHAD)**

Mix the nuts, sugar and Orange Blossom Water in a small bowl. Layer between the Knaifi as above and proceed to baking.

This traditional Cheese Filling may be used as an alternate filling to the nuts, if preferred.
Cheese Filling:

2	**16 OZ. CONTAINERS RICOTTA CHEESE (WHOLE MILK)**
1	**CUP SUGAR, MORE OR LESS TO TASTE**
1/2	**CUP HEAVY CREAM**

In a 3 qt. bowl, mix the Ricotta cheese, sugar and cream and blend well. Use as a filling for the Knaifi and continue layering and baking as above.

Cook's Notes: Knaifi phyllo dough can be found at all Middle Eastern stores in the freezer case near the phyllo dough.

To blanch pistachios, shell and pour boiling water over them. Steep the nuts for a few minutes before draining and cooling. Peel the skins by rubbing them. Let dry before using. Blanched pistachios are also available at Middle Eastern markets.

My Sister Elaine's best friend, Arlene, loved her grandmother's Knaifi. Over time, Arlene's mother made this "Western" version using shredded wheat instead of the Knaifi pastry and topped with the basic sugar syrup. Much to Arlene's delight, her mother would sometimes add chopped walnuts to the top of the cream filling before finishing the dish.

ARLENE'S SHREDDED WHEAT DESSERT
KNAIFI'T ARLENE

Cream Filling:

6	CUPS MILK (DIVIDED USE)
2	CUPS HEAVY CREAM (PINT)
1	12 OZ. CAN EVAPORATED MILK
2/3	CUP SEMOLINA (SMEDE) OR FARINA (NOT QUICK-COOK VARIETY)
8	TABLESPOONS SUGAR
	PREPARED SUGAR SYRUP (SHIRREH) BASICS, PAGE 6 - COLD - TO TASTE

In a 5 qt. pan, heat 4 cups of the milk with the cream and evaporated milk over medium heat. Before the milk comes to a boil, add the semolina or farina gradually and stir. Then add the sugar, stirring constantly until it thickens to a pudding consistency. Pour into a 3 qt. glass bowl and set aside to cool. Then cover and refrigerate until firm.

Optional Walnut Topping for the cream filling or as a substitute for the filling:

2	CUPS CHOPPED WALNUTS
3	TABLESPOONS SUGAR
1/2	TEASPOON CINNAMON

Mix the walnuts, sugar and cinnamon in a small bowl and set aside.

Arlene's Shredded Wheat Dessert

Preheat the oven to 350 degrees.
Prepare the "Western" Knaifi

3/4	LB. SWEET BUTTER, MELTED (DIVIDED USE)
18	SHREDDED WHEATS (LARGE)
2	CUPS WARM MILK (OR MORE IF NEEDED)

Remove the cream mixture from the refrigerator and set aside. Grease the bottom of a 9" x 13" x 2" rectangular glass or metal pan with some of the melted butter.

Warm 2 cups of the milk in a 2 qt. glass bowl in the microwave. Soak the shredded wheat (one at a time) in the warm milk for a few seconds. Remove and gently shake the excess milk out of each one. Separate them and place them in the baking pan, pressing together and down to form a uniform bottom layer.

Top this layer with the cream filling. Sprinkle the optional nut topping, if desired. Repeat the same soaking procedure for the top layer of shredded wheat. Gently press down on this top layer when completed. Drizzle the reserved melted butter over the top of the entire pastry and bake for 15 to 20 minutes.

Remove the pastry from the oven and generously spoon the cold, prepared sugar syrup over the top of the pastry. Set aside to cool somewhat and cut into squares to serve. Refrigerate any leftovers. This may be warmed for approximately 30 seconds in the microwave before serving again.

Cook's Notes: This cream filling can also be used as a substitute for the cheese filling in Sitto Naima's Shredded Pastry (Knaifi) recipe on page 151.

I loved early December because we always celebrated the feast day of St. Barbara. Sitto would make Sleetah for the whole family. This wonderful wheat dessert would be decorated with lots of spices, fruits, nuts and raisins. Then Sitto would light a candle on top and we would all sing to St. Barbara. She was a young Arab girl who was martyred because of her faith. It was a sad story, but we always loved the dish that remembered her and cherished our traditions.

WHOLE WHEAT DESSERT
SLEETAH

1	LB. WHOLE GRAIN WHEAT BERRIES (HINTA)
8	CUPS COLD WATER

Sort and rinse the wheat. Place in a 3 qt. glass bowl, cover with cold water and soak overnight. Then pour out the soaking water into a measuring cup, adding enough water to make 8 cups.

In a large 6 qt. pot, bring the wheat and water to a boil. Cover, lower to a simmer and cook for about 1 to 2 hours until tender. Check to make sure the water is not absorbed, adding more water if necessary.

While the wheat cooks, measure out the following:

1/2	CUP SUGAR, OR MORE TO TASTE
2 1/2	TEASPOONS WHOLE FENNEL SEEDS, FRESH GROUND
2 1/2	TEASPOONS WHOLE ANISE SEEDS, FRESH GROUND
1 1/2	TEASPOONS CINNAMON
1/2	CUP GOLDEN RAISINS
1/2	CUP DARK RAISINS
1	CUP TOASTED WALNUTS, COARSELY CHOPPED
1	POMEGRANTE, PEELED, ARILS (SEEDS) REMOVED AND SET ASIDE
1/4	CUP ANISE CANDY (OPTIONAL)

In a small cup, mix the sugar, the ground fennel, ground anise and cinnamon together to blend.

Whole Wheat Dessert

When the wheat is cooked it should be open, but firm, and have a slight chew to it. Drain any remaining liquid and immediately add the golden and dark raisins and stir to mix through. Add the sugar and spice mixture, then spoon it all onto a large serving platter.

Top the mounded wheat with the walnuts, pomegranate seeds and anise candy over all. if preferred, sprinkle a bit more sugar over the top or sprinkle over individual servings, to taste.

Cook's Notes: Frequent stirring of grains makes them starchy and sticky. Only check the bottom of the pan and the water content.

The pomegranate is integral to the dish. The tart-sweet seeds are a great contrast to the sweet wheat, raisins and nuts.

Anise candy is available at Middle Eastern and Asian stores.

Easy Halvah

Halvah is so popular throughout the Middle East and it is now main-stream in the west. My grandmother always had some in the refrigerator and my sweet tooth always craved it. I can't help but wonder what Sitto would think of this modern version of Halvah that I created. It will be loved by the children, but don't tell them that the Tahini is good for them or that you didn't work too hard making it!

EASY HALVAH
HALAWEH SAHIL

1	16 OZ. JAR TAHINI (UNBLENDED)
1/2	CUP PREPARED SUGAR SYRUP (SHIRREH) BASICS, PAGE 6
1/3	CUP HONEY, OR TO TASTE
1/3	CUP SESAME SEEDS

Pour out the excess sesame oil accumulated at the top of the tahini jar and reserve. Refrigerate for later use in a recipe calling for sesame oil.

Grind the sesame seeds in a blender or processor and add the tahini.

Set aside a glass 8" x 8" x 2" square baking pan or dish.

In a 3 qt. pan, heat the prepared sugar syrup to boiling and lower to a simmer. If the syrup is already thick, proceed with the recipe. If the syrup is thin, continue to simmer until the syrup is 34 degrees or the soft ball stage. (See Cook's Notes.) Then add the honey and simmer for a minute to blend.

Remove from the heat and pour into the food processor over the tahini mixture. Process until the mixture is well blended, with no lumps and it appears smooth.

Pour into the ungreased pan. Smooth out evenly with a spatula or a large spoon to about 1 1/2" thickness. Cool and then cut into squares. Serve at room temperature or cover with plastic wrap.

Cook's Notes: Some more modern versions of Halvah contain chocolate marbling. A favorite melted chocolate may be mixed into the tahini mixture immediately after you spoon it into the glass pan. With a butter knife, create marbling through the mixture. Do not completely mix into the chocolate.

Favorite nuts, such as chopped, blanched pistachios may also be added to the mixture right before spooning it into the glass pan.

Another option: Toasted or plain sesame seeds may be sprinkled on top of the hot mixture after it has been removed from the heat and spooned into the glass pan. Press into the top of the mixture with a spatula.

The oil at the top of the tahini is to be removed in order for the ratio to work properly. I have found that blended products do not work for this recipe. The tahini will be firm and almost solid once the oil is removed. Some oil will be an inherent part of the tahini and that will be fine.

Soft ball stage:
If the syrup is hot enough, a 1/2 teaspoon of it dropped into a glass of cold water will form a soft ball.

To blanch pistachios:
Shell and pour boiling water over them. Steep the nuts for a few minutes before draining and cooling. Peel the skins by rubbing them. Let dry. Middle Eastern markets carry blanched pistachio nuts.

Our best times together were when I helped Sitto shell nuts on the kitchen table. We'd talk about anything, much of which I can no longer remember. Now that I, too, am a grandmother, I can't help but wish I had asked her more about her life and her remembrances of Aleppo. I now realize that spending time with our grandparents and learning their history are the gifts that we should treasure.

ALMOND HALVAH
HALAWEH LOZ

2	CUPS ALMONDS, WHOLE, RAW
1	16 OZ. JAR OR CAN TAHINI
1	CUP HONEY

Almond Halvah

Process the almonds to a fine grind in a food processor.

Pour out the excess sesame oil accumulated at the top of the tahini jar and reserve. (Use later in a salad dressing or a recipe calling for sesame oil.)

Heat the tahini and honey for a minute or more on the stovetop or in the microwave. Stir to blend. Pour it into the ground almonds in the processor. Process, then pulse until it's completely mixed together and looks like dough.

Immediately remove it to a loaf pan or an 8" x 8" glass pan. Press down and smooth the mixture and allow it to cool. Invert onto a plate before slicing.

Cook's Notes: As an option, any chopped nuts, like pistachios or more almonds, can be added to the mix after removing it from the processor. Fold the nuts into the warm mixture and then press into the pan. Toasted sesame seeds may also be added to the top as a garnish. Even a layer of melted chocolate makes it special!

May be stored at room temperature or refrigerated.

Sitto made this traditional Syrian pudding often and I know it was one of her favorites. I do remember that she sometimes added a layer of Jell-O to the top of the chilled pudding, for a kind of double-decker approach. She had truly "Americanized" her country's pudding with that touch!

CORNSTARCH PUDDING
M'HALLABIYA

1/3	CUP CORNSTARCH
1/4	CUP SUGAR PLUS 1 TABLESPOON
1/4	TEASPOON SALT
3	CUPS MILK (DIVIDED USE)
1	TEASPOON ORANGE BLOSSOM WATER (MAHZAHAD)
	PISTACHIO NUTS, BLANCHED, CHOPPED (OPTIONAL)

Cornstarch Pudding Layered with Cherry Jell-O

Cornstarch Pudding

Combine the cornstarch, sugar and salt in a small 1 qt. bowl. Gradually stir in 1/2 cup of the cold milk, mixing to ensure that the cornstarch is well blended and there are no lumps.

Pour the remaining milk into a 2 qt. saucepan over medium heat. Slowly add the cornstarch mixture while continually stirring. Simmer over low heat, stirring until thickened. The pudding will thicken enough to coat the back of a spoon. Do not bring to a boil. When it has thickened, remove from the heat and add the Orange Blossom Water and stir to mix in well.

Pour into small glass serving dishes or parfait glasses and chill.

To serve traditionally: Sprinkle the chilled pudding with chopped blanched pistachio nuts.

Sitto's topping: Prepare cherry Jell-O according to package directions and pour onto the top of the cooled pudding and chill again.

My favorite updated topping: Serve the chilled pudding topped with canned, drained mandarin oranges, which have been splashed with 1/2 teaspoon of Orange Blossom Water.

Another non-traditional option: Top the chilled pudding with any fruit compote or fruit preserve.

Cook's Notes: Some have preferred Rose Water as a flavoring for this pudding. In our family, we have consistently used the Orange Blossom Water. Try both and decide for yourself.

To blanch pistachios: Shell and pour boiling water over them. Steep the nuts for a few minutes before draining and cooling. Peel the skins by rubbing them. Let dry. Blanched nuts are also available at Middle Eastern markets.

Sitto often served this traditional Syrian fruit roll, called Amardeen, when I was young. She'd buy it at the Syrian grocer and I remember it would be wrapped in cellophane with Arabic writing on it. It was much loved by everyone and always a part of every dessert table, to be served with Arab coffee.

This homemade version is fresher-tasting, with no preservatives, and it's surprisingly easy to do. A sauce pan, food processor, lipped baking sheet and a low-heat oven are all you need. The young and old will enjoy these healthier traditional fruit rolls. Tear off a piece and enjoy!

APRICOT FRUIT ROLL
AMARDEEN

4	CUPS DRIED APRICOTS, QUARTERED, RINSED
1	CUP WATER
2/3	CUP SUGAR
	JUICE OF HALF A LEMON
1/4	CUP ORANGE JUICE
1	TABLESPOON ORANGE BLOSSOM WATER (MAHZAHAD)

Apricot Fruit Roll

Place the apricots in a covered pan with water, bring to a boil and lower to a simmer for 10 to 15 minutes.

Puree the apricot mixture in a food processor and return to the pan. Add the sugar, lemon and orange juice and simmer for 5 to 10 minutes to thicken. Taste and adjust the sugar, if needed. It should be sweet but tart.

Remove from the heat and add the Orange Blossom Water. Preheat the oven to 150 to 170 degrees.

Spray a lipped 12" x 16" baking pan with Pam and then cover with plastic wrap. Pour the mixture into the baking pan over the plastic wrap and bake overnight or for 7 hours, keeping the oven door ajar during this time. The finished fruit roll will be somewhat dry but sticky to the touch and with a leather-like look.
Cool and slice or roll up in the plastic wrap to store for later.

Many years ago, as a little girl, I remember Sitto's hospitality when friends would drop by. I can still see the chairs all around the living room...with Sitto pulling out her best serving pieces. Offering sweets, she'd say, "tfaddalu" in Arabic, coaxing each one to try this or that.

But, the most vivid memory I have is of a tray of dried fruits that Sitto would offer. They were simply done and considered a delicacy to these newly-arrived immigrants. The dates would be prepared in several ways, with nuts or sweet fillings, rolled in sugar and beautifully presented on decorative trays or Depression glass plates that she considered "for company." These many years later, it is such a vivid reminder of those humble cooks and what they considered the best sweets of their home country, Syria.

Dates Four Ways

DATES FOUR WAYS
AJWEH HELOU

Place the dates in a shallow dish and sprinkle with about 2 tablespoons of water on them. Microwave for about 40 seconds. Let them cool for a few minutes and peel the skin off of them. Then make a slit on one side. Remove the pit and proceed with the recipe.

Dates with sweetened yogurt cheese, cream cheese or goat cheese - Open the split date and put about a teaspoon of the cheese in it. Serve as is, warm in an oven or simply roll in granulated sugar.

Dates with whole almond - Place a raw, peeled whole almond in the top of each date and roll in granulated sugar and serve. Another option is to roll the dates in shredded coconut instead of granulated sugar after filling.

Dates with ground walnuts - Fill the date with a mixture of finely ground walnuts, sugar and a teaspoon of orange blossom or Rose Water.

Date balls - After microwaving the dates, remove the pits and then mash into a paste. Add chopped walnuts and form into balls about an inch in diameter.

Cook's Notes: Serve any of the dates on a beautiful platter, just like Sitto did years ago!

Sitto was so proud of her "company" serving pieces. As a youngster, I was charmed by those serving dishes! They'd have lovely little forks attached for presenting sweets...so typical of the times! Thinking back, I now realize how frugal and resourceful they were in preparing and serving these dried fruits!

APRICOTS IN SYRUP
MISHMOSH B'SHRREH

1	CUP DRIED APRICOTS, RINSED
2	CUPS COLD WATER
1/2	CUP SUGAR, OR MORE TO TASTE
1	TABLESPOON LEMON JUICE
1	TABLESPOON ORANGE BLOSSOM WATER (MAHZAHAD)
2	WHOLE CLOVES

Apricots in Syrup

Soak the apricots in water for several hours overnight.

Remove the apricots and set aside, reserving the soaking water. Pour the soaking water into a saucepan, add the sugar, lemon juice and cloves and bring to a boil.

Lower the heat, add the apricots and simmer on low for 30 minutes. Add the Orange Blossom Water at the end and set aside to cool in the pan.

The apricots may be served in syrup or as stuffed apricots.

To stuff the apricots, remove the drained apricots and fill with a teaspoon of sweetened yogurt cheese (page 17) or honeyed yogurt. Drizzle the syrup overall.

My father-in-law taught us how to pan-roast chestnuts and they became a great treat at our house on a winter's evening. The children always looked forward to peeling back the salty shell and sinking their teeth into the smooth and buttery cooked chestnuts.

PAN-ROASTED CHESTNUTS
KASTANI

1	LB. FRESH CHESTNUTS
1/2	CUP WATER
3	TABLESPOONS SALT

Wash the chestnuts in cold water and dry. Make an X cut into the flat side of the chestnut with a chestnut cutter or carefully, with a sharp knife.

In a measuring cup, mix the water and salt together until blended.

Place the chestnuts into a large 12" sauté or fry pan in a single layer and cover. Heat the chestnuts over a low flame until they are brown on one side. Then turn each chestnut over and pour the water/salt mixture over them. Cover again.

The chestnuts will continue to cook as the salt water begins to evaporate. When the salt water has completely evaporated, stir them until all of the chestnuts are dry and coated with the salt. Test one to be sure they are tender. The finished chestnuts will have a soft and creamy texture, not mealy.

Serve warm in individual serving bowls.

Cook's Notes: A chestnut cutter is now available from major kitchen stores. It will easily and safely make an X cut into the flat side of the chestnut.

Pan-Roasted Chestnuts

ALMOND CRESCENTS
LOZ HILAL

8	OZ. ALMONDS, NATURAL, WHOLE
1	CUP POWDERED SUGAR
1/2	TEASPOON CARDAMOM, GROUND
3	TABLESPOONS ORANGE BLOSSOM WATER (MAHZAHAD)
1	EGG, BEATEN
1/2	CUP TOASTED SESAME SEEDS
1/2	CUP SLICED NATURAL ALMONDS, COARSELY CHOPPED

Pulse the almonds in a food processor to a fine grain. Add the sugar, cardamom and Orange Blossom Water until it all binds together.

Form the entire mixture into 1" balls. Then roll all into finger shapes about 2" long and set aside on a flat plate or work surface.

Put the beaten egg, sesame seeds and chopped almonds into 3 separate bowls.

Preheat the oven to 350 degrees.

Prepare a baking pan or sheet with a silicone pad or parchment paper.

Dip each finger-shaped mixture into the beaten egg and replace on the plate or work surface.

Dip each finger-shaped mixture into either the sesame seeds or chopped almonds. Then place each one on the baking sheet and form into a crescent shape by curving each end inward.

Bake for 10 to 12 minutes. Makes about 30 crescents, depending on the size.

Store in a tightly closed container.

Cook's Notes: Since the egg wash and the toppings make for messy hands and fingers, preparing them in these steps makes it much easier.

These crescents can also be made completely with one of the two toppings, rather than half and half. Rose Water may be substituted for the Orange Blossom Water as a flavoring, if preferred.

This cookie is flourless and so, for a more moist result, bake for only 10 minutes.

BEVERAGES

When I was a little girl, my grandmother had regular calling days. The ladies in her circle would designate a different day of the week in which their homes would be open to impromptu visits by friends and acquaintances. Every Thursday afternoon, Sitto's house was usually found with her friends around the kitchen table as I rushed in from school.

As I think back, I realize what a charming Victorian tradition she and her friends had brought with them from Syria. Since these visits were rarely prearranged, it never ceased to amaze me how quickly Sitto could reach into her refrigerator or pantry and would create a lovely afternoon offering for her friends. On a hot July day, nothing was more tantalizing than her homemade orangeade drink. She would take the homemade orange nectar concentrate she had prepared from the refrigerator. Sitto would pour the orange nectar to about 1/4 of the bottom of a tall glass, add water and ice and we would all sit down to chat in the back yard under the big old pear tree. It was more delicious than any juice drink or soda you could find then or now and so much more healthful!

SITTO'S ORANGEADE
SHARAB BURDQAN MIN SITTO

12	ORANGES
6	LEMONS
2	CUPS SUGAR, GRANULATED, OR MORE TO TASTE

Juice the oranges and lemons, straining to remove the pits.

Pour into a 3 qt. saucepan with the sugar. Simmer the juices and sugar until slightly thickened, for about 10 or 15 minutes. During the simmering, taste and adjust for sweetness. If the oranges are very tart, the sugar may need to be increased.

Sitto's Orangeade

Cool, put into a sealed container or glassware and refrigerate.

To serve:

In an 8 oz. glass, pour the concentrated nectar up to 1/4 of the bottom of the glass, depending on the sweetness desired. Add water and ice to fill. Stir and enjoy!

Cook's Notes: The simmered nectar will appear thinner when hot, but will thicken when cooled. It should be thinner than syrup.

Summer picnics and backyard barbeques were usually accompanied by a pitcher of home-made lemonade. A quick alternative to store-bought lemonade can be easily made with the basic Sugar Syrup, Shirreh, as a base for the squeezed fresh lemons.

LEMONADE
SHARAB LAIMUN

1	CUP PREPARED SUGAR SYRUP (SHIRREH) BASICS, PAGE 6
1	CUP LEMON JUICE (ABOUT 6 TO 8 FRESH LEMONS)
	COLD WATER
	ICE
	FRESH MINT LEAVES, OPTIONAL

Combine the sugar syrup and lemon juice in a 2 qt. pitcher. Add the water and ice and mix. Taste and add more syrup, if desired.

Garnish with fresh mint leaves. This recipe makes approximately 12 servings.

Single Serving:

3	TABLESPOONS PREPARED SUGAR SYRUP (SHIRREH) OR TO TASTE - BASICS, PAGE 6
2 - 3	TABLESPOONS LEMON JUICE (1 LEMON)
	WATER AND ICE

Combine the sugar syrup and lemon juice in a tall glass. Fill with cold water and ice. Taste, adjust if needed and enjoy!

Soon after arriving in America, my grandmother's eldest brother, Naim, married. Although Aunt (Khali) Waheeda is a vague memory for me, I do recall that she loved rose jelly. This was her specialty, which she lovingly made from the roses in her own garden. As a youngster, I couldn't acquire a taste for it. Later, I would note that the older people would enjoy rosewater drinks on a hot day, much like they did in Aleppo. Today, it would be a wonderfully exotic drink, which you may wish to embellish, even with a few rose petals.

ROSE WATER COCKTAIL
SHARAB MA'WARD

2	TABLESPOONS PREPARED SUGAR SYRUP (SHIRREH) BASICS, PAGE 6
1	TABLESPOON ROSE WATER, OR TO TASTE
	GRENADINE SYRUP OR DROP OF RED FOOD COLORING
	WATER AND ICE

In a tall glass, add the sugar syrup and Rose Water flavoring. Fill with cold water, stir and adjust, adding more syrup or Rose Water to taste.

Then add the Grenadine for color. Add the ice and garnish with rose petals.

Cook's Notes: If using rose petal garnish, remember to use only fresh roses which have not been sprayed with any pesticides.

Those wishing to add spirits to this drink will find it is a great base for a cocktail.

Some people prefer using Orange Blossom Water instead. If so, substitute it for the Rose Water and Grenadine syrup. Garnish with orange slices and fresh mint.

Rosewater Cocktail
Photo courtesy of The Gilded Bellini

Arab Coffee

Those wonderful evenings with family and friends always included Arab coffee. As a little girl, I watched as the guests drank the last bit of Arab coffee and turned the cup over onto the saucer. I loved this exciting tradition of "reading" the coffee cups. Invariably, one of the women would be 'versed' in telling fortunes by looking into the cups. They'd chat for a few more minutes and then, one by one, the reader would turn their cups upright and tell their fortunes. Oh, what a wondrous thing for a young girl to watch! The thick Qahwa would coat the cup in interesting patterns, denoting "mountains," "trips," "gifts," "new arrivals" and such. The grown-ups would be exclaiming their surprise, with laughter and hopeful smiles. Although I was too young to drink the coffee, I could still be part of the mystery of fortune telling!

ARAB COFFEE
QAHWA ARABY

12	OZ. WATER
2	TABLESPOONS TURKISH PULVERIZED COFFEE
2	TABLESPOONS SUGAR, OPTIONAL, ACCORDING TO TASTE
4	DEMITASSE OR MINIATURE COFFEE CUPS
1/4	TEASPOON FRESHLY GROUND CARDAMOM (OPTIONAL)

Heat the water to boiling in a long-handled brass Turkish coffee pot or "briq." Lower the heat and slowly add the coffee and stir to blend. Bring to a boil again over high heat, watching carefully, as it may boil over. When the foam appears, skim the foam off with a serving spoon into the demitasse cups.

Return the coffee pot to the heat and add the sugar and cardamom, per individual taste. Stir and then heat again while watching it so that it doesn't boil over. Simmer for a few minutes more.

Remove from the heat and pour into the foam-bottomed cups. The foam will rise to the top. Do not stir and wait a minute or two until the grounds sink to the bottom of the cup before drinking. Serves 4.

Cook's Notes: The coffee and sugar amount will vary based on individual taste. A few tries will yield your favorite ratio.

Both the brass coffee pot ("Kanakha" or "briq") and the ground Turkish coffee are readily available at any Middle Eastern store.

A small saucepan will do in a pinch.

Some grocers grind the coffee along with cardamom.

Arab Coffee, Reading the Cups

THE MELKITES AND THE EARLY CHURCH

The Melkite story goes back to the dawn of Christian history in Antioch, Syria. In 64 B.C., this major capital city in the Eastern Roman Empire became the important east-west trade route. With a large and diverse populace, it was the site of the beginnings of the Christian Church. The Melkites were originally part of the apostolic church of Antioch, founded in that city by St. Peter himself, before he journeyed to Rome. It began with the preaching of the Apostles, Peter and Paul, who followed Jesus' command to his followers. The first converts were Jews, but all nationalities followed: Romans, Greeks, Syrians, Egyptians, Africans and others throughout the Roman Empire. These first converts of the apostles were known as "Christians."

Antioch, in turn, passed this faith on to the neighboring regions and became the "mother" Church of Syria, as Alexandria was for Egypt and Rome was for the West. Jerusalem, the cradle of Christianity itself, was regarded as the "Mother of all the Churches." When Constantinople was added in the 4th Century, it was as the new capitol of the Eastern Roman Empire.

In the 4th and 5th Centuries, a deep divide arose over the nature of Jesus. The Church Of Antioch held to the faith that Jesus has two natures, fully human and fully divine. The Emperor at Constantinople, who stood as the head of all those Eastern Christians, taught this belief. Those Syrians and Lebanese who followed the lead of the Emperor were dubbed Melkites or "King's Men," from the Syriac word for king, which is "Malko" or "Malek" in Arabic. It was originally used as a pejorative term but was later adopted by the Melkites themselves.

The great schism over the nature of Jesus split the Church of Antioch into two factions: the Orthodox (Melkite) faction, which believed that Jesus was both human and divine and the Jacobite faction, which adhered to Jesus' nature as solely divine. Their following formed the Jacobite Church of Syria, the Coptic Church of Egypt and the Gregorian Armenian Church.

By the late fifth century, six great liturgical families, or Rites, had emerged. A rite is a distinct and characteristic style of Christian living used by a local Church to express its faith through local customs, traditions and liturgical ceremonies. These rites spread beyond the mother churches, becoming part of the great spiritual heritage of the entire church. Six main rites of the Catholic Church are:

- The Roman Rite, practiced through most of the Western Church
- The Antiochene Rite, practiced in Syria and Palestine
- The Chaldean or East Syrian Rite, practiced in the Mesopotamian and Persian Churches
- The Coptic Rite, derived from the Church of Alexandria and practiced throughout the Egyptian Patriarchate
- The Armenian Rite, practiced in Armenia
- The Byzantine Rite, practiced by the Melkite Church, originated in the new capital of the Roman Empire - Byzantium or Constantinople. It's the most practiced Eastern Rite followed by Albanians, Bulgarians, Greeks, Byelorussians, Carpatho-Russians, Georgians, Hungarians, Italo-Greeks, Rumanians, Russians, Slovaks and Ukranians.

From the seventh century onwards, the Patriarchate of Antioch was the battleground of the Middle East. Persians, Arabs, Crusaders and Turks struggled for control of this territory. These invaders persecuted the Melkites because of their Christian faith and their allegiance to the Byzantine Emperor. As the persecution increased, the Melkite patriarchs were forced to live in exile, usually in the imperial city of Constantinople. And for this reason, the Melkites of today, descended from those fifth-century champions of the faith, now worship in the Byzantine Rite rather than the Antioch Rite.

The separation between Rome and Constantinople and the Crusades caused the link between the Melkites and the Catholic West to be disrupted. When the Turks conquered the Byzantine Empire in 1453, they established their own capitol in the former imperial city and the Melkites' connection with Constantinople increased. The conquerors considered being a Turk and being a Muslim, one and the same thing. Christians were not only members of a different faith, but of a different nation (millet) as well. Each Christian church formed a separate millet, subject to the authority of its Patriarch, even in what we would today consider civil affairs. Since the Melkites were already well within the Byzantine orbit, the Turks made them subject to the Patriarch of Constantinople, a situation that was to persist for many years.

Despite the isolation imposed by the Turks, there were several points of contact with the West, especially in Syria. From 1625, Roman Rite missionaries entered the Middle East under the patronage of the French consulates. These priests served in Melkite churches with the local clergy for many years, establishing ties between Antioch and Rome. Melkite Bishop Eftimios Saifi, Archbishop of Tyre and Sidon, gathered many priests favorable to union with Rome and formed them into a community. Also at the time, a number of Melkites were pursuing studies in the West and were also favorable to this union.

From 1672 to 1724, there had been several bishops, each with their respective supporters, vying for the patriarchal dignity. In 1724, a divide in the Melkite Church occurred. Before his death, Patriarch Athanasius III recommended a Greek monk named Sylvester to succeed him. However, the clergy and people of Damascus elected Seraphim Tanas as Patriarch Cyril VI. Cyril, who had studied in Rome, sent his profession of the Catholic faith to the Pope in Rome. The Greek Patriarch then confirmed the choice of Sylvester and so the Melkites were definitely divided. Since that time there have been two lines of Melkite Patriarchs of Antioch: the Catholic followers of Cyril and the Orthodox successors of Sylvester.

Eastern Rite Catholics did not come to the United States in any number before 1870. In the late 19th century and early 20th century, many Melkites who immigrated to the United States and Latin America were determined to retain their culture, although their reasons for immigration were not religious. The movement also included members of most of the religious groups in the Middle East at that time, such as the Orthodox, Maronites, Protestants and Muslims.

The arrival of Syrian and Lebanese immigrants toward the turn of the twentieth century was principally for economic reasons. The poverty-torn Middle East, still under the Turks, had little to offer these people. America was in the midst of its great industrial expansion and people were coming to work in the mills and factories. Most of these new arrivals settled on the East Coast of the United States, principally in the mill towns and industrial centers of New England, New York and New Jersey. In time, many immigrants chose to move westward, establishing colonies in various large cities throughout the United States. They formed the first parishes and communities of worship with the help of Middle Eastern priests. Although they functioned under Latin (Roman) rite bishops, great cooperation was attained in the formation of these parishes. The first Melkite parish in America, St. Joseph's in Lawrence, MA, had its beginnings in 1896. After that date several more parishes were established, the majority between 1910 and 1930.

After the Maronites, the Melkite Catholic Church is the largest and most prosperous Catholic community in the Middle East, mainly in Syria, Lebanon, Israel, the West Bank and Jordan. Today, in the West, there are 42 Melkite Catholic parishes in the United States. The Diocese of Newton, MA includes 38 parishes and 28,000 members. In

Canada, the Diocese of Saint-Sauveur de Montreal has 12 parishes and 43,000 faithful. In Sydney, Australia, the diocese of St. Michael's of Sydney has nine parishes for 45,000 Melkite Catholics. There is also a parish in London. In total, membership includes more than 1.5 million faithful.

Some Catholics today may question the idea of maintaining Eastern churches here in the United States and may feel that the Melkite Catholic Church is for those who won't assimilate. But these churches of the Byzantine Rite are not "national churches tied to the language or tradition of any one foreign country." The international Byzantine Rite, being Greek in origin, does not even point to its Near East ancestry but to the universality of the Church. Today, the Melkites hold a special place in the Church and the entire Christian world.

Archbishop Neophytos Edeby of Aleppo, Syria, had once stated the need for Eastern Catholics in the midst of the church: "We are here in the first place to bear witness to the effective Catholicity of the church, to proclaim publicly that Catholicism is truly universal, that it respects and assimilates everything in the most diverse civilizations that can be regarded as of spiritual value." He also stated, "We are here to show that no one group can monopolize the Church and that we are all brothers, children of the same mother. In refusing to allow themselves to be "Romanized," Eastern Christians are not being merely parochial or sticking to outdated traditions. They know they are being faithful to a mission, a vocation, which they cannot deny without being untrue to themselves...."

GLOSSARY

It should be noted that most items in this glossary are in English with the Arabic pronunciation in italics. When the Arabic is noted first, it is because this is only found in Middle Eastern cooking and through the stores specializing in such.

Aleppo Pepper: This sweet and sharp chile from the Aleppo region of Syria has a moderate heat that doesn't overpower its fruity flavor. If unavailable, use paprika or red pepper flakes. *Fil Fil Ahmar Halaby*

Allspice: The whole berry of the pimento bush is the size of a large pea and has a deep rich brown color. Clove and peppery flavors are very pronounced, especially when ground fresh. *Bahar*

Anise Seed: This small seed has a wonderful sweetness and hints of licorice flavors. Grind for breads, biscuits and tea. *Yansoon*

Bois De Panama: Also see Soapwort. It is a pale dry wood from the Quillaja Saponaria tree. When soaked and boiled in water, its saponins produce thick white foam used to make Nataef for Karrabij. In the U.S. it can be found in Health and Herbal Stores and on-line. See the "Where To Buy It" section of this book.

Bulgar: Hulled wheat, steamed until partly cooked and then dried. It is ground in fine, medium and coarse grades. It has a nut-like flavor. *Burghul*

Cardamom Seed: The extracted seeds from whole green, white or brown pods. This seed should be ground only as needed, since it loses most of its flavor within days of being ground. Available as whole seeds or ground, it is used for Arab coffee and cakes. *Hal*

Chestnuts: This nut is native to the Mediterranean regions. A rare treat, east or west, it can be cooked or pureed. *Khastani*

Chickpeas: These legumes are sold dried and must be soaked before cooking. They are also available as canned. Use them in dips, in Hummus, roasted, cooked with grains, even candy-covered. They are also known as Garbanzo beans or Ceci. *Hummus*

Cinnamon: The dried aromatic inner bark of certain tropical Asian trees in the genus Cinnamomum. It loses flavor quickly, so fresh ground is best. *Qurfi*

Clarified butter: Butter is heated in order to render and separate the milk solids and water from butterfat. Used for its distinctive flavor in main dishes and specifically for certain pastries in Syria and the Middle East. It will not burn when sautéed, so it is very useful in browning nuts and preparing recipes. *Zibdi M'Dataha or Semneh*

Coriander Seed: The dried seeds from the Cilantro herb plant. It has a strong, savory aroma with light hints of citrus when ground. *Kizbara*

Cream of Tartar: Originally discovered by the French, this is actually a byproduct of the wine making process. Tartaric acid forms inside the fermenting casks into a white crystalline substance. The French found that this is not only a souring agent, but also a stabilizer for whipped egg whites and frostings.

Cumin Seed: A dried herb in the parsley family and similar in looks to caraway. The seed is pungent, sharp and distinctively bitter. *Kemoon*

Datah: A Syrian blend of spices, also known as Baharat, consisting of ground cinnamon, nutmeg, black pepper, cardamom, allspice and cloves. Paprika may be added for color. It is distinctly stronger than allspice and more complex. This blend, on page 62, varies in the Middle East and is used extensively in Syrian cooking.

Dibis: This is a "molasses" like syrup. Tamarind is the typical ingredient used in the Aleppo type, sometimes combined with pomegranate. *Dibis Rumman*

Fennel Seed: This small green seed can be used whole or crushed for a wonderful complexity of flavor, sweet, with a hint of licorice. *Shumrah*

Grape Leaves: Prevalent in all of the Middle East, the vines are grown for the leaves rather than the grapes. Blanched, they are then filled, rolled and cooked in lemon and spices. Aleppo cooks serve them hot rather than chilled. *Waraq Enab*

Halvah: A Middle Eastern treat made with ground sesame seeds, honey and sometimes almonds or pistachio nuts. It is pressure-cooked and is available in Middle Eastern and mainstream markets. It has high nutritive value. *Halaweh*

Knaifi: Shredded pastry dough used in making pastries, similar to phyllo, made by forcing it through a fine metal plate. This pastry is available in most frozen food cases of Middle Eastern stores.

Kosher Salt: A unique process to salt, the "diamond" process adds a bit of puff to the salt crystals. This makes it the perfect salt for staying in suspension with blends of other spices and in cooking. *Milh*

Lemon Salt: Citric Acid, also known as Sour Salt, dissolves nicely and adds the taste of lemon while preventing crystallization in syrups. It contains a natural acidic ingredient found in all citrus fruits and is used in canning to keep foods from discoloring. This does not contain salt. *Milh Laimun*

Mahlab: The pale hard kernels from inside the pit of the wild small black cherry tree. It has a slightly almond sweet and spicy flavor with a faint floral note for pastries and breads, available as whole kernels or ground.

Nigella: Tiny black seeds from the Nigella Sativa flower with a pungent taste. Also known as black cumin seed. Used extensively as a flavoring in Syrian Cheese and *Kahek*. *Habet Baraka*

Olive Oil: The oil of pressed olives, the first pressing is termed "Extra Virgin Olive Oil." It is used extensively in Syria, where sesame oil is not readily available. *Zait*

Orange Blossom Water: Produced from the blossom of the sour Orange Tree, it lends a delicate perfume to pastries, puddings and syrups. *Mahzahad*

Phyllo: Very thin pastry-dough sheets used in baking appetizers and sweets. *Waraq*

Pine Nuts: Also called Pignolia nuts, they are the kernels from the cones of the Umbrella pine in the Mediterranean Region. Pine nuts are cream colored and evenly oval. *Sanobar*

Pomegranate Seed: The juicy, shiny pink seeds of the fresh fruit. Use the seeds as a garnish for many Syrian dishes and salads. *Rumman*

Rose Water: The distilled essence of culinary-grade rose petals can add a perfume to drinks and syrups of the Middle East. *Ma'ward*

Saffron: It is the stamen of the crocus flower and is the most expensive spice in the world. 70,000 of these flowers must be hand picked to produce one pound. It has a powerful flavor for rice and provides a deep yellow-orange color. The threads are crushed with the back of a teaspoon and mixed with a little hot water before using. *Asfar*

Semolina is a fine yellow grain derived from hard durum wheat and used in Middle Eastern baking. It is not to be confused with Semolina flour, which is a finer grain used in making pasta. Some recipes may use farina (not the quick-cooking variety) in place of the Semolina, but only where specified. *Smede*

Sesame Oil: Prized in the Middle East as the oil of choice. It is the oil obtained from the pressing of sesame seeds. *Zait Simsom*

Sesame Seeds: The pale cream seeds of a tropical plant. They are oily and highly nutritious. They can be found in baked dishes, in *Zahtar* spice mixture, in Tahini and as the main ingredient in *Halvah*. *Simsom*

Soapwort: Root of the Saponaria Officinalis, grown in the Middle East and Europe. It is crushed, soaked and boiled to produce Saponin, a foam in making *Nataef* for *Karrabij*. (Also see Bois de Panama) This perennial plant with a thick taproot is a member of the clove family with a soapy consistency. It is also called Soapbark. Used in herbal medicines, teas and making soaps. See the Where To Buy It Section of this book. *Er el Halawa*

Spearmint: The prevalent mint in the Middle East. It is used in fresh and dried forms. Peppermint is more readi- ly available and is often substituted. *Nanat*

Sumac: This ground reddish berry of the Sumac shrub has a pleasant fruity taste, sweet and slightly bitter with a sour flavor similar to lemon. Sumac is used to make *Zahtar*. *Sumahq*

Tahini: A thick oily paste made of toasted ground sesame seeds. It is used from a jar as a topping, like peanut butter, in Hummus or cooked in certain dishes. *Tahina*

Tamarind: The brown pulp from the Tamarind tree is used to make a tangy, sour-sweet syrup. When cooked with sugar, it produces molasses-like syrup that is the mainstay condiment used in many Aleppo dishes. It is also produced as a popular drink in the Middle East. The syrup keeps for more than a year, with no need to refrigerate. Tamarind is also called "Date of India." *Tamar Hindi*

Thyme: A perennial herb, grown in the Mediterranean having a subtle, "minty" flavor with woody stems and small green-gray leaves. The fresh whole sprigs are sold in bunches or the leaves are removed and dried, discarding the stems. *Zahtar*

Tumeric: A pungent, slightly bitter and peppery spice, similar to mustard. Its active ingredient is curcumin. This is often used in place of Saffron for yellow coloring. *Kurkum*

Zahtar: A varied mixture of Middle Eastern herbs including thyme and sumac mixed with salt and sesame seeds. Brick or green colored with the green being more popular in Aleppo, Syria. See page 45.

WHERE TO BUY IT

Middle Eastern Grocers

Andre International Gourmet Food
1478 West Spring Valley
Richardson, TX 75080-6502
972-644-7644
www.andrefood.com

Bulk Foods
3040 Hill Avenue
Toledo, OH 43607-2931
888-285-5266
www.bulkfoods.com

Buy Arabic On-Line
www.buyarabic.com

Dayna's Market
26300 Ford Road, Ste. 407
Dearborn Heights, MI 48127-2854
313-999-1980
www.daynasmarket.com

Fattal's Syrian Bakery and Grocery
975 Main Street
Paterson, NJ 07503-2323
973-742-7125
www.fattals.com

George's Middle-East Market
368 Getty Avenue
Paterson, NJ 07503 973-278-1771

Halalco Supermarket
155 Hillwood Avenue
Falls Church, VA 22046-2913
703-532-3202
www.halalco.com

Jordan Market
24771 Alicia Parkway, Ste. A
Laguna Hills, CA 92653-4618
949-770-3111
www.jordanmarket.com

Kalustyan's
123 Lexington Avenue
New York, NY 10016-8120
212-685-3451
www.kalustyans.com

Mountain Rose Herbs
P.O. Box 50220
Eugene, OR 97405
800-879-3337 / 510-217-4012 (fax)
www.mountainroseherbs.com
For Soapwort Root

My Spice Sage
877-890-5244
www.myspicesage.com

Natco On-Line
www.natco-online.com

Njaim Mid-East Food Centre
1010 Belfast Road
Ottawa, Ontario
Canada K1G4A2
613-244-2525

Nouri Brothers Syrian Bakery
999 Main Street
Paterson, NJ 07503-2224
973-279-2388

Old Chatham Sheepherding Company
155 Shaker Museum Road
Old Chatham, NY 12136-2603
www.oldchathamsheepherding.com

Parthenon Foods
9131 W. Cleveland Ave
West Allis, WI 53227-3436
877-301-5522
www.parthenonfoods.com

Penzeys Spices Many Retail Stores
800-741-7787
www.penzeys.com

Redco Foods, Inc.
P.O. Box 879
Windsor, CT 06095-0897
www.junketdesserts.com

Sahadi Importing Company
187 Atlantic Ave
Brooklyn, NY 11201-5605
718-624-4550
www.sahadis.com

Shamra Grocery
2650 University Blvd
Wheaton, MD 20906
301-942-9726 www.shamra.com

Sausage Supplies/Casings
www.sausagemaker.com

Sultan's Delight
7128 5th Ave
Brooklyn, NY 11209
800-852-5046

Todaro Brothers
555 2nd Avenue
New York City, NY 10016
212-532-0633
www.todarobros.com

Whole Spice
1364 N. McDowell Blvd., Ste. 20
Petaluma, CA 94954-1115
707-778-1750
www.wholespice.com

Zamouri Spices
P.O. Box 65
Olathe, KS 66051-0065
866-329-5988
www.zamourispices.com

BIBLIOGRAPHY

Alan Davidson, The Case Of The Foaming Root: Los Angeles Times, December 1, 1994

The Melkite Exarchate, Melkites in America, A Directory and Information Handbook, 1971

Archimandrite Cyril Anid, I Grew With Them, Memoirs of 45 years of parish work at St. Ann's Melkite Church, Paterson, NJ, Jounieh, Lebanon: The Paulist Press, 1967

Note: St. Ann's Melkite Catholic Church is now located at 802 Rifle Camp Road, Woodland Park, NJ. 07424
www.saintannmelkitechurch.com

INDEX
RECIPES - ENGLISH

(v) Denotes Vegetarian

INDEX
RECIPES - ARABIC

Printed in the USA
CPSIA information can be obtained
at www.ICGtesting.com
LVHW071627250823
756182LV00032B/653

9 780578 689357